STAR SPANGLED SOCCER

PLAYING AND COACHING
THE AMERICAN WAY

by Terry Fisher

Cover Photo: DON HUSTON

Soccer for Americans
Box 836
Manhattan Beach, California 90266

DEDICATION

To my parents, who gave me the freedom to grow
To Al Miller, who gave me the determined spirit to succeed
and
To my wife, who shares all my burdens, willingly and with love

Cover Design: Mike Faye
Artwork: Ron Norris
Typesetting: Century Composing
1770 Magnolia, Long Beach, California

PUBLISHER'S PREFACE

It will be at least twenty more years before soccer historians can sit back and evaluate the era of 1965-1980 in American soccer. While little change has occurred in the game in other countries, except for the triumphs and failures in World Cup competition, such is not the case in America.

Foreign coaches, players, teams, and even referees have influenced us. An American style occasionally pokes its head around the corner, but at the slightest reversal retreats to the darkness and safety of the "tried and true." Skills and technique are now emerging, but far from world-class caliber. The best 12 year olds in the world, we now know, are probably not in America.

With American growth must come leadership, and a confidence that "we can do it at home, with our own talent." Terry Fisher is home-grown, aggressive, sensible, and sensitive about soccer. His teams play hard, clean soccer, the players have been fairly treated, and are encouraged along positive lines. He has worked as a player and as a coach through the American system, if there is one, and will be a leader in tomorrow's game.

STAR SPANGLED SOCCER is about coaching and how players fit into learning patterns in the sport. It offers hints, insights, and challenges into coaching and playing. It teaches players and coaches to create and to think before the moment of decision on the field. This book is much needed at a time when many are "doing" soccer, but not enough are "thinking" it. Who should read it? We think that everyone who is serious about American soccer should.

"Everyone Plays" is the motto of the American Youth Soccer Organization. Young players need organizers who develop the "maximum play" concept, such as "six-a-side" competition.

TABLE OF CONTENTS

The American setting has included bringing in many of the world's top stars. Here, two of the masters, George Best and Pele, meet for the first time.

CHAPTER ONE

THE AMERICAN SETTING . . . A FEW THOUGHTS

THE AMERICAN SETTING . . . A FEW THOUGHTS

Though soccer has grown, and millions now play, the United States is in no way a soccer power today. We provide no threat to such leading soccer nations as Germany, Holland, England, Brazil, or Argentina. "Second World" countries like Sweden, Mexico, Bulgaria, Russia, and Spain could also defeat our national team on a regular basis. At the moment we are equal with Switzerland, Canada, Luxembourg, Denmark, and the Caribbean countries, along with most of the African Federation. One could even make the point, rather convincingly, that we are not progressing at all, since there were times when the United States performed well in World Cup and Olympic competitions.

Great opportunities exist in America, and factors which will contribute to our eventual success include:

1. The low cost of soccer programs. Many other sporting activities in high schools and colleges are being curtailed due to high costs. Economically, one of soccer's most obvious benefits is its low-cost of operation. Nothing will change that.

2. Schools, which have held soccer back for many years, are now offering better programs, with teachers and coaches better qualified.

3. Young players everywhere now look up to the North American Soccer League, both for inspiration in playing and as they dream about future stardom. All of us must exert pressure on the league and on these teams to play the American player, providing him with needed experience.

Standardization

Soccer is not exactly the same everywhere. I know of no other sport where the rules (laws) have been tampered with as in soccer. We must seek a common refereeing system at all levels, in order to aid players *and* referees. High schools and colleges should limit the number of substitutes to five or less. This would allow for continuity of play, and encourage more planning by coaches. Senior level soccer (any non-professional player over 19 plays it) is the next big game in America, and these leagues should conform in every way to FIFA regulations.

The FIFA World Cup. All countries compete under the same set of laws. (Copyright, FIFA, Zurich.)

2

Coaching Responsibilities

Coaching is only one small aspect of what the American coach must do. Even in youth soccer, the coach must take on new responsibilities in promotion and in revenue-producing activities. At UCLA we were able to convince our athletic director to reinvest gate receipts directly into the soccer program. Promoters sometimes make good coaches, but coaches should always be good promoters. I know no high school or college coach who was ever dismissed for not winning games, but some should be dismissed for not promoting the game. We must create an atmosphere where people will want to be a part of serious American soccer.

Part of coaching should be an awareness of what sells soccer. "Crazy George" has added spice to the San Jose soccer experience.

America's National Youth Team

When the Coca Cola International Youth Tournament was announced by FIFA in 1975, the optimists immediately expected the United States, with the best youth players in the world, to dominate and to pave the way for the World Cup. Our National Youth Team, with players 19 and under, has performed with limited success. We have been well-organized, physically strong, and have entered competitions with simple game plans. Though on occasions the teams have been hastily put together, consistent and qualified coaching has prepared the players for the rigors of international competition. Psychological preparation and goal-scoring abilities continue to emerge as our glaring weakness. It may be several years before we see magic with the ball and scores favoring the American youth squads.

3

The Youth Programs

The most gratifying fact about youth soccer is the number of talented and selfless organizers, coaches, and referees. They are eager to learn, sympathetic with the players' problems in developing a modicum of skill, and have conformed to plans set forth by national bodies.

Unfortunately, this conformity works against the full development of the player. The "under 10" soccer player is cheated in America. He is overcoached, he under-plays, and is engaged in a Mini-World Cup atmosphere, with full fields, teams, trophies, and a full complement of supportive parents who look only at the game score. Young players should play on small fields, with six-a-side competition. Truncated fields and added touches to the ball will help develop a flair for the game, a quality almost totally lacking in America. But, I believe it will come!

Sadly, youngsters in America refuse to play soccer without supervision. Only rarely do I see "soccer for soccer's sake", impromptu games without adults. It is ironic that youth soccer programs could not have existed without the selfless giving from well-meaning parents. Yet, the player who will excel is the one who spends those hours alone with the ball, "on his own". Real play, in the true sense of the word, is missing with American youth.

In Tegucigalpa, Honduras, the fans line up the see the Americans play. In this 1978 youth tournament, our showing was a disappointment.

4

Indoor Soccer

The North American Soccer League has wrestled with indoor soccer for a number of years, and is now committed to a full winter schedule. Little is known about the game, except that it is rough, fast, goal-producing, and possibly more attractive to the American spectator. Players have many opportunities, though less space, for showing their skills. I recommend closely-supervised play indoors, both for conditioning, variety, and skill work. It may be someday that America emerges as the indoor capitol of the soccer world, and it could be more popular than the outdoor game!

Indoor soccer first gained a foothold here when the Moscow Red Army team played the Philadelphia Atoms team in 1974.

The World Cup

It is possible for a country to be successful in soccer without winning the World Cup. Yet, countless restless and unrealistic Americans are pointing to the 1982 World Cup in Spain as something which is within reach. While the expanded number of entries will now allow two countries from our Confederation, qualification will still be difficult. We are still a few years away from seriously challenging our neighbor, Mexico. Soccer must be a Spring sport in the colleges, and our top athletes in high schools must be attracted to the game. When this happens, America's fortunes in World Cup and Olympic competition will be secure. Here are the steps to the top:

INTERNATIONAL EXPERIENCE   (We're getting it)

A SERIOUS CHALLENGE   (Not yet)

QUALIFICATION   (Possible, at best)·

WINNING THE WORLD CUP   (The rest of the world is improving, too)

At the present, we are down the list of soccer's nations, with at least 50 countries with equal or superior teams representing their best. So, now that we are ready to accept some facts about where we are today, let's think seriously about American soccer, and find out how we can change ourselves and our players.

Technique is developed during practice sessions, sometimes alone and sometimes in small groups.

CHAPTER TWO

TECHNIQUE

TECHNIQUE

A player must have the ability to control the ball at all times during soccer competition. Since the game is fluid the player must be able to control the ball at variable speed, always with opponents nearby. From lack of effectiveness technique limits the options of a soccer player. Improving technique makes a more efficient and dangerous player. We try to improve technique in three various stages:

    1.) **Fundamental** - no running, but half efforts with emphasis on understanding the required movements of the body in relation to the ball.

    2.) **Match Related** - tying together the individual technique learned in stage one and movement in a game with light pressure.

    3.) **Match Conditions** - advancing to utilization of the learned technique in real game situations. Everyone can do it in practice, but can they do it in the game?

Teaching technique requires exactness of demonstration, patience for practice, and confidence and total credibility of the players as to its importance in the game. "Why should I improve?", think many self-satisfied players! Learning technique requires the athlete to concentrate on body and ball movement. This exercise in concentration is a great aid to the player's mental development towards the game. Concentration throughout the 90 minutes should be everyone's goal, thus reducing errors and inefficiency. The techniques worth consideration are:

    1) Ball Control - juggling and receiving the ball - trapping
    2) Kicking - shooting - passing
    3) Heading
    4) Dribbling
    5) Tackling - screening
    6) Throw-ins
    7) Feinting
    8) Goalkeeping

Ball control, here with the outside of the foot, allows the attacker many more options.

Ball control — "by whatever name you wish to use"

Being able to put the ball where you want it and the ability to instantly control it are two of the greatest essentials in the game. This is ball control. All players must realize that the human body and the ball need to be synchronized for efficient movements. Players who cannot play the ball accurately nor control it quickly will soon be passed by in favor of players who can. The game is all about accuracy, speed, and efficiency. Mastering the body and the ball simultaneously is the key to success.

Players are not born with ball control — they must acquire it through long hours of repetition and dedication. Young amateurs and senior professionals alike must spend countless hours on improving their ball control.

Body Surfaces

Head
Chest   **All must be comfortable with the ball.**
Thigh
Feet

The great unknown in a game is where the ball will be played, in what position we will be in when the ball arrives to us, and under what pressure we will be from our opponents. So, we must train for all of these circumstances.

Good ball control requires balance and coordination. Intercept the ball with your body, using whichever surface is required. Get your body behind the ball. Have your body surface meet the ball and relax the surface at the moment of impact to cushion or collect the ball. Withdrawing the body surface will take the pace (speed) off the ball and allow the ball to be easily played.

BALL JUGGLING

Perfect harmony between body and ball — keeping the ball in the air and under control, precise, controlled rhythm of ball and body. No one runs the length of the field juggling the soccer ball. However, ball juggling is an effective way of acquiring a feel for the ball — a touch so essential to successful playing in all regards. Ball juggling utilizes all body surfaces individually and collectively.

Instep of the foot
Inside of the foot
Outside of the foot
Thighs
Chest
Head and shoulders

Elementary jugglers will find even the most simple movement difficult. Have patience and be determined. Try this:

Hold the ball in your hands and drop it or toss it into the selected surface—i.e. - juggle the ball once and catch it. Toss it again and juggle 1 - 2 and catch it— toss it again and juggle 1 - 2 - 3 and catch it— and so on up the points where you are challenged. Whenever the ball drops out of control and hits the ground start over again. Toss and juggle 1 catch— etc. 1 - 2 catch.

9

PROGRAMMED JUGGLING

As you become more highly skilled it is necessary to challenge your imagination with ball juggling routines involving sophisticated patterns that demand absolute control of the ball.

Examples

1) Right foot only
2) Left foot only
3) Alternating right and left foot
4) Thighs only
5) Head only
6) Feet and thighs only
7) Feet and head only
8) Thighs and head only
9) Right foot, left foot, right thigh, left thigh, head and back down
10) Right foot, head, left foot, right thigh-left thigh-head, repeat
11) All combinations — two juggles on each foot, thigh, head, etc.

WITH TWO PLAYERS

Players of equal ability should pair off, competing against one another.

Team juggling:
Example— Heading ball to other line-sprint to opposite end of line.

ₓx x x x — 5 yds. — x x x x

PRESSURE TRAINING FOR BALL CONTROL

3 players   2 balls   (4 players if you add opposition for (B)

A   B   C
                           20 yds.

|◄━━━━━━━━━━━━━━   ━━━━━━━━━━━━━━►|

A & C Servers

B   Working

Duration: 30 seconds to 2 minutes

"A" serves short 3 yd. ball to "B" who has run towards "A" and controls ball on his head for two touches and serves back to "A". "B" turns and sprints toward "C" who serves the ball to head, to chest, to thighs, or to feet. Wherever the ball comes "B", he controls with two touches and returns an accurate pass. Repeat. Switch.

Proper kicking starts with using stationary balls. Here a goalkeeper takes a goal kick in an Earthquake-Aztec game. Goalkeepers should take all goal kicks.

Kicking

A kick is a continuous series of movements, all of which are interrelated and easily identifiable. A kick consists of (1) the position taken to the ball by the kicker, (2) the pendulum of the kicking leg— backwards and forwards, (3) the point of impact and (4) the follow-through. When these four basic mechanics of the kick are correct, they significantly increase the possibility of the accuracy of the kick.

1) Kicking must be mastered with all surfaces of the foot.
   Inside of the foot
   Instep of the foot
   Outside of the foot
   Heel

2) If we desire the ball to stay low we must strike it on slightly above the center of the ball. If we want high we need to strike it below the center. The lower on the ball we strike it and with increasing velocity— the greater the degree of height achieved on the ball.

3) Kicking in a game takes only three forms:
   A.) Clearances— The ball is played away with reckless abandon, usually by the defense simply to stop a dangerous thrust by the opponent. Not very graceful, but very effective.
   B.) Passes— The ball links teammates together in an invisible net. The most essential weapon to insure good team play and possession of the ball.
   C.) Shooting— The most undercoached, neglected skill in the game.

11

Clearances

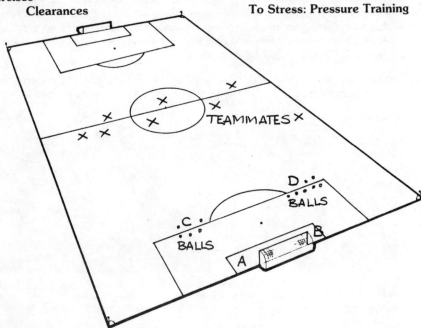

C and D roll or bounce balls to A and B— A clears C and B clears D— looking for distance and height. When A and B have cleared ball they run around goalposts to other side and clear a second ball first time. Their teammates try to control the cleared ball out of the air. If they do they get a point (competition).

10 balls each side or 30 seconds to two minutes.

Clearances

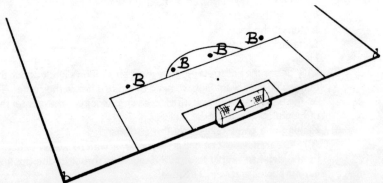

18 yards or more (depending on age and ability). "A" is on the goal line— Teammates (B) asked to shoot accurately on goal requiring "A" to clear balls (without using hands) first time, preventing a goal.

Passing

There is an invisible web which links every player on the team. The web is one of cooperation, understanding, and selflessness. It implies a willingness to give up the ball, to pass it, but the receiver must do something with it. The passer has the expectation that it will return if the opportunity presents itself. The qualities of a good pass are timing, accuracy, and weight (can it be controlled).

The pass means that "You and I (the team) can do more if I don't have the ball at this moment." Each player should learn that the variety and frequency of passes is infinite.

50 yard square— 6 vs. 6   to no goals

Exercise
To Stress:
Accuracy
Passing Angles
Pace of Pass
Timing
Deception
Team Work

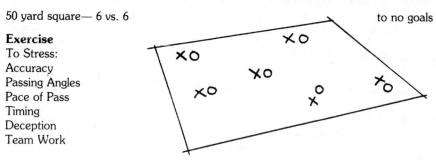

6 versus 6— 15 minutes— two teams fighting to keep possession inside a confined area. Teaches importance of good passing, running to support teammates off the ball, concentration and fitness.

All variations possible. Increase or decrease area, according to number of players and ability.

Exercise

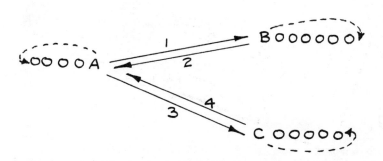

13

3 lines— one ball

A pass to B— to A— to C to A. Run to end of own line. One or two touch— distance— 5-20 yards.

How many variations can you think of in this exercise? In practice, how many variations can your players think of?

Exercise
3 players— 2 balls— Pace of Pass

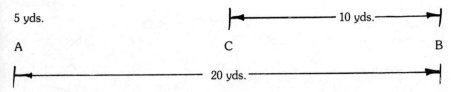

5 yds.

A   C   B

|← ———————— 10 yds. ————————→|

|← ———————————— 20 yds. ———————————→|

C runs to A, returns the ball 5 yards, turns and sprints to half way mark and returns 10 yards. The pass to B will start the exercise anew. Time: 30 seconds to 2 minutes.

Exercise
To Stress: Vision, Alertness

|←— 10 YRD —→|

10 Y

6 cones— 5 players— 1 ball

Players pass balls among themselves— they one-touch and run to the unoccupied cone.

14

Exercise

Chip Pass— Lofted Pass

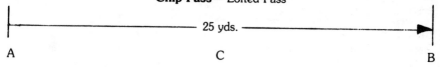

A	C	B

A chips ball to B
A and C exchange places (C   A   B)
B chips to C
A and B exchange places (C   B   A)
C chips to A
C and B exchange places (B   C   A)

Continuous movement and accurate passes a must!

Exercise

Volley Pass

3 players— 2 balls

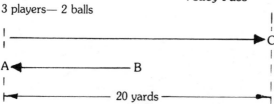

B runs to A and returns service with inside of foot volley— turns, runs to C and returns instep volley. Repeat for 30 seconds to 1 minute.

Passing in games is almost always under pressure.

15

A   B   C

A must pass ball through spread legs of B to C. C returns ball to A through legs of B. B must always face passer. Passers may change locations for variety, also varying the distance.

When we discuss passing we must remember that to be effective we must meet the pass. It may sometimes be necessary to pass the ball backwards in order to keep possession. The best pass is a simple, early, disguised, accurate one to a teammate. No one has ever said that all passes must be toward the opponent's goal.

Long Passes
Full field

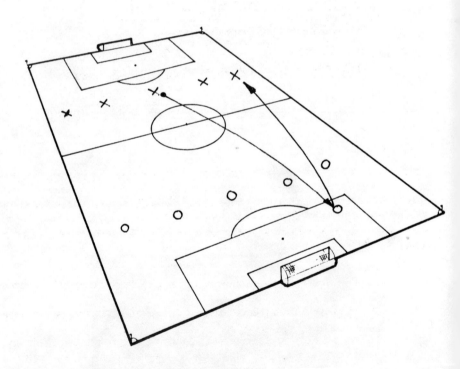

Team X tries to drive ball over goal line with long passes— if they do they score a point. Team O tries to prevent this by collecting ball and sending long passes into end defended by Team X. 20 minutes. Hint: Have players search for an imaginary "teammate" on the opposition to receive the pass.

The final result of good shooting.

Shooting

Effective shooting is the most important part of attacking play. Developing first rate goal scorers should be extremely high on your check-list for a successful team. When a team creates a high percentage scoring opportunity through effective team play it is very discouraging to see a goal shot go wide of the mark or even missed entirely. Good shooting must be developed through rigorous training, emphasizing the need for "quick release" of the shot.

Hints for Your Team:

(1)   There are times when a shot needs to be powerful and times when it needs to be accurate.

(2)   There are greater chances of success for shots which are low and to the far post (playing the angles).

(3)   Many times a goalkeeper will not handle cleanly the initial shot and rewards can be reaped from following the original shot to the goalmouth.

(4)   Great goalscorers are incisive in their actions, deadly in their strike and unmerciful in their will to score.

(5)   Today every player within the team must have the ability to shoot and score.

(6)   Shooting from within 6 yards or from 30 yards all must be practiced, and with a moving ball.

Shooting exercises

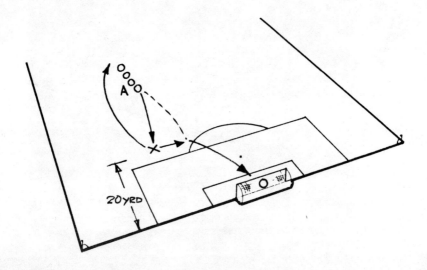

A passes to X for a wall pass— A shoots, first timing the ball.

A becomes X— X goes to end of line.

Combinations

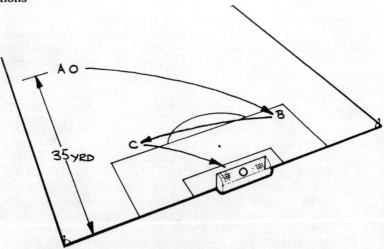

A chips to B who first times ball across 18 yard box to C who shoots first time.

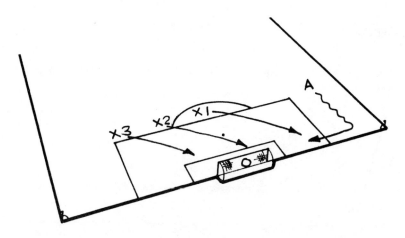

"A" is winger who dribbles to end line and crosses ball to X^1 who has run near post, X^2 who has central and X^3 who has run the far post. X^1 X^2 X^3 must run to those spots to create chance for the other to finish. Ball is played in air or on ground by first player to receive it.

Seldom does the player have the chance to shoot uncontested.

Pressure Training

X is cone— O sprints right and shoots. Sprints back around cone and shoots with other foot. Sprints back around cone and shoots with right foot. Repeat 1 minute. May use open goal for maximum success.

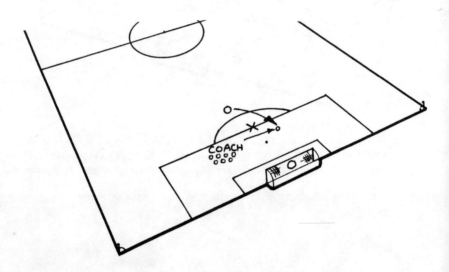

Coach serves balls into penalty area. X must fight off challenge of O and get in a goal shot as quickly as possible.

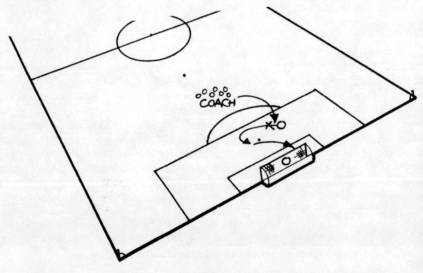

A swings ball to #2 who plays the ball back to #3 who shoots first time.

B swings ball to #1 who plays the ball back to #3 who shoots first time.

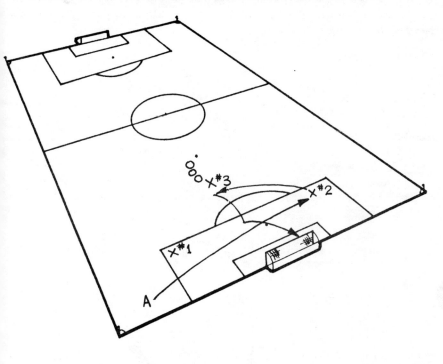

Heading

The unique and somewhat unusual skill of heading belongs only to soccer. We utilize the head to control, pass, clear (defend), or to score (attack). To do any of these we must feel confident in our ability to use our head as a weapon. Young players must be taught to overcome the fear of striking the ball with their head. Strike it on the hairline, eyes open, mouth closed and arms used for balance. Obtain power in the header by arching the back and snapping the neck, head, and upper body forward. Senior players must recognize that failing to be a good header of a ball is very costly in many pressure situations. Physical size is not always important, and can be overcome with proper jumping technique. Players must be taught to time their jump for the ball. Developing power in the legs to improve your vertical jump is very important. Players who are outclassed physically must learn to outmaneuver larger players by intelligent positional play. Decide on the flight of the ball and intercept it in the air before it reaches your opponent by attacking the ball. Select the shortest distance and get there first. Defenders should try to avoid jumping flat footed for the header. Stand back of the attacker and run into the jump for extra height and power.

Being able to score goals with the head is a dangerous and valuable asset. Head balls down and away from goalkeepers. Sometimes power is needed. Otherwise, only the slightest flick of the ball will change its direction, and will score you the game winner.

Heading to control

Exercise

2 players   1 ball

A   B

5 yds

A and B heading back and forth— 2 touch— control and head back— Coaching point: on the second touch the player must leave the ground and head ball back. Improves heading power.

Practice

Partner standing with ball held in hands in front of his body above his head. Partner must jump and head stationary ball 25 times without pause.

Heading to Pass

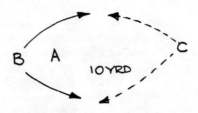

A tosses to C— B runs right or left and C heads to B. Accuracy is important. The heading pass must be to a target.

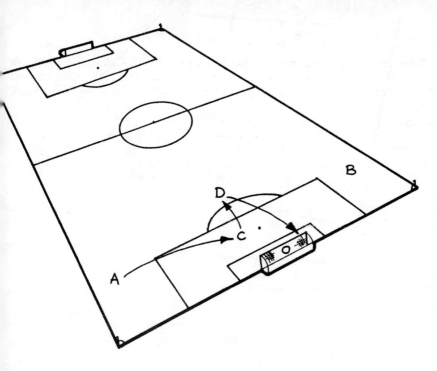

Alternating crosses from A and B, to C who heads ball down for D to score. For advanced players, put in defensive player versus C.

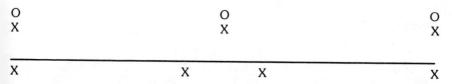

Goals kicks (Practice)— defenders head ball to midfielders who continue play 3 versus 3— with one large goal use GK— with small goal, no GK.

Heading to Clear
3 players

A   B   C

             5 yds

C tosses ball to A who heads back to C over B, who gives passive challenge to A.

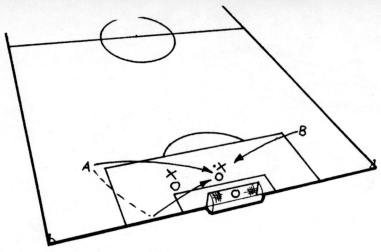

Goalkeeper
2 Defenders— 2 attackers
A and B cross balls from wings
O's must head balls clear, X's must go for goal.

Exercise

Goalkeeper punts or throws ball

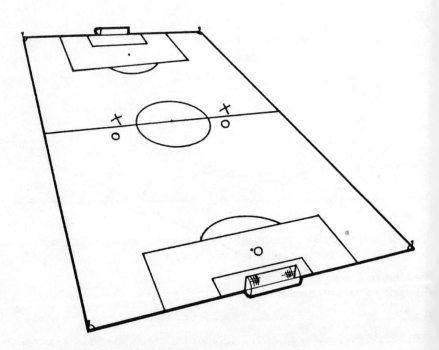

X's and O's challenge for punted or thrown ball.

24

Heading— Soccer Tennis. (Head only)

2 teams— heading over crossbar

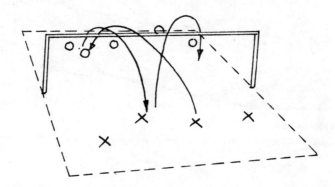

To Score

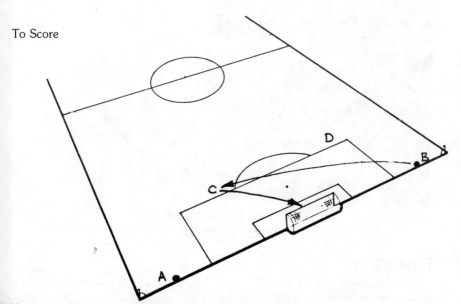

Alternating Side— chipped balls from 25 yards— Accurate

A to D   B to C— Head and score— follow up the shots.

The key to scoring goals with your head is (1) early crosses from your teammates, (2) ntelligent runs to open spaces, and (3) attacking the ball. Try to head balls down and away from goalkeeper.

The dribble means "I've got it, I'm keeping it, and you may get it if you get open."

Dribbling

When you cannot pass the ball to a teammate it is necessary to keep the ball under close control by dribbling. Good dribblers have the skill to manipulate the ball under the tightest of circumstances in order to maintain possession.

Good dribbling technique requires that you keep the ball within playing distance. Keep your eyes up so you can see the field of action around you, be able to change speed and direction instantly with the ball. Good dribbling technique is whatever is working for you. Even Pele had an unorthodox dribbling style— but it worked! Develop your style and be comfortable.

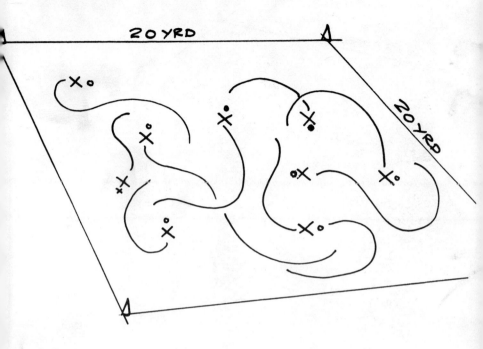

Dribbling in and out of one another without crowding. Eyes up, change speed, change direction. Intervals 2-3 minutes. Many changes of direction. Change balls at signal from coach.

Variations

1.) Players try to touch other players' ball with a light touch or tackle.

2.) Several players don't have a ball and try to secure one from another player.

3.) Coach removes one ball from game just before each signal. At signal, player who does not have a ball when switching takes place is out.

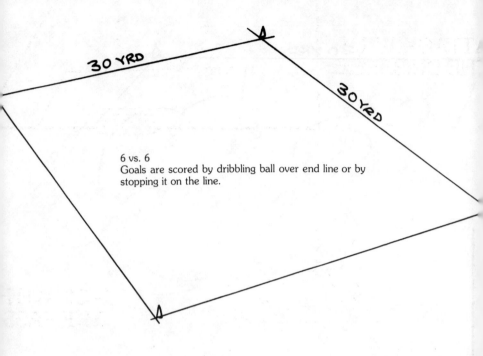

6 vs. 6
Goals are scored by dribbling ball over end line or by
stopping it on the line.

Dribbling in the game is a last resort. If a pass could be made to accomplish the same
result, pass it. Less effort is required and passing puts more pressure on the defense—
keep the ball rolling. Remember dribbling takes time— don't over dribble. An easy
formula to remember as you decide whether to dribble or pass in attack is:

NUMERICAL ADVANTAGE

Attack with the dribble, and commit defenders

NUMERICAL DISADVANTAGE

Attack with the pass

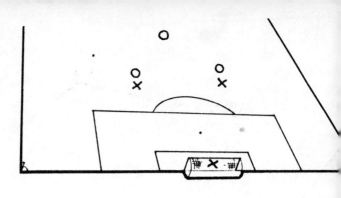

ATTACK WITH THE DRIBBLE!

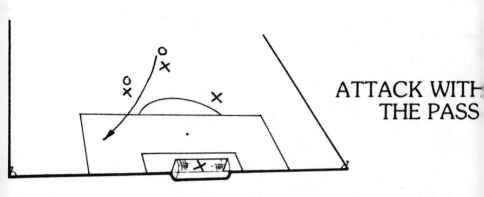

ATTACK WITH THE PASS

Dribbling
4 players

A   CD   B

20 yds

A and B spread legs as goals— extra balls at their sides.

C and D play 1 versus 1 inside A and B.

When goal is scored or goes past A or B another ball is immediately in play.

1 - 3 minutes intervals— this intense work teaches agressiveness in tackling and individuality in dribbling and attacking.

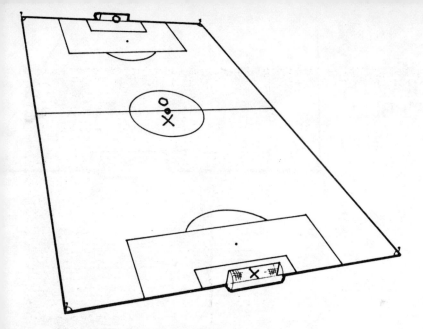

1 versus 1 full field— played till goal is scored or ball goes out of bounds— kick in—
develops stamina and determination. Only one minute.

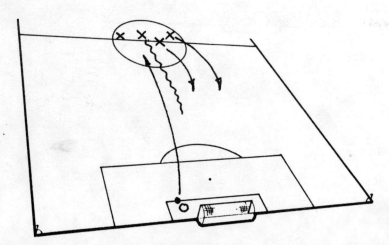

Goalkeeper takes goalkick to center circle 4 players try to control ball— whoever
controls plays 1 versus 3— dribbling to get ball to goal and shoot and score versus GK.
Game played till goal or ball out of bounds.

Teaches: Determination
Control
Shooting

Screening the ball. One of the best ways of retaining possession.

Screening

Closely aligned to dribbling is *screening* which simply means placing your body between the ball and the opponent to make it more difficult, and hopefully impossible, for him to tackle the ball. Good screening is a fundamental requirement for teams to keep possession— you are buying time until you can either advance with the dribble, or pass. Remember you must keep the ball within playing distance so you are not called for obstruction.

Screening and Dribbling

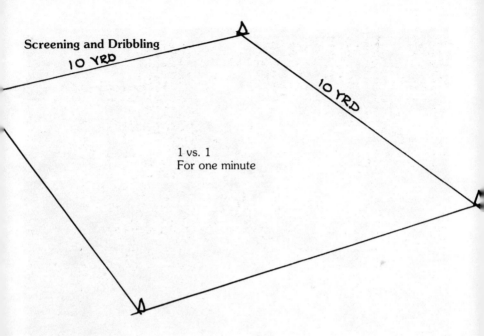

10 YRD

10 YRD

1 vs. 1
For one minute

Don't let opponent touch the ball.

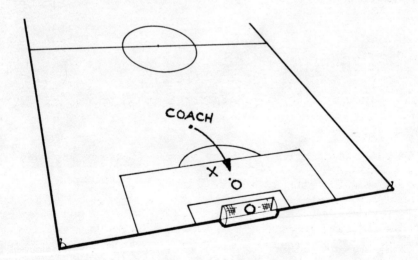

COACH

X

O

Serve ball in box to X, who must dribble and screen and get off a shot within specified time (10 seconds).

The tackle must be done from a position of strength, and while fully balanced.

Tackling

A team wins possession of the ball through interception (anticipating good passes or receiving bad passes) or by fighting it away from his opponent with his feet by tackling. Just as effective dribbling requires skill, timing, power and deception— so does tackling. To effectively challenge for the ball the player closes down the distance between himself and the opponent, proceeding *cautiously* and under control for the final two yards. Do not dive in or lunge at the ball. Force your opponent to one side– right or left. This will allow you an opportunity to reduce the attacker's alternatives. Force the attacking player towards your supporting teammates or towards the boundaries of the playing field. Try and force the attacker to make a mistake with the ball. All you need is a momentary loss of control and this is the moment to strike. With quick reactions, and the body balanced, lower the body to a semi-crouched position and use the largest surface area of your foot possible. Pull through the center of the ball.

The sliding tackle

This is a last resort because it commits you to a position on the ground and temporarily out of the flow of the game. Moreover, it can be dangerous to the tackler and the opponent as well. This tackle is usually made from a side angle opposite the ball. The tackler bends his support leg and thrusts his tackling leg in front of the dribbler. Keep your eyes on the ball.

The perfectly-executed feint, where the player has moved in one direction while the attacker goes around him.

Feinting

In order to play soccer successfully we need to oftentimes deceive the opponent and make him do things that will make our intended action possible. There are only two types of feints:

    1.)   Without the ball
    2.)   With the ball

Both of these types require agility and quickness, and patience in your practice. To make the feint effective the player making the feint must already know what his second move is going to be. How well the feint is "sold" will determine the success of the next move. Feints without the ball allow us space to gain advantage to receive the ball or for a teammate to gain an advantage.

Feints with the ball are more successful when adequate skill accompanies the body swerve, thus enabling you to control the ball and body.

Exercises

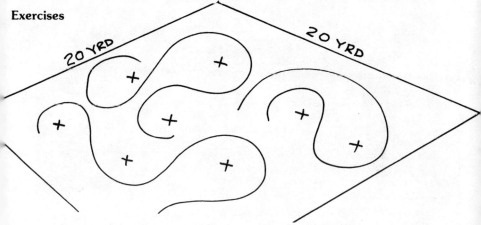

Players must swerve in and out of one another changing speed and direction. Do it with a ball.

Exercises
Slalom races— with/without ball

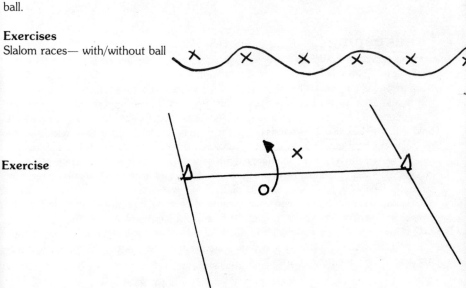

Exercise

Opposing players try to cross line into opponent's territory without being tagged.

35

In the USA's training camp in the hills outside of Tegucigalpa, Honduras, two of America's goalies train. John Benbow (left) and Jim Tietjens know the value of helping one another, even they are competitors for the same position.

Goalkeeping

Goalkeepers are invariably credited with the success or failure of a team. A good goalkeeper lifts the performance of the team or shatters the good efforts of an entire team through faulty play. Goalkeepers are the last line of the defense and the first line of the attack. They are equally important in initiating goal scoring opportunities as they are in preventing them. Great responsibility is placed on every goalkeeper. The goalkeeper is unique in that he can use his hands within the penalty area to save and handle the ball. He may also be required to leave the penalty area in desperate situations to clear a ball with a kick or win it with a tackle. Goalkeepers are generally larger than the average player. A goalkeeper's weight should be in proportion to his height in an effort to utilize maximum strength, flexibility, quickness and stamina.

Goalkeepers need to possess a high degree of courage, composure, confidence, and concentration. Weaknesses in any of these areas will be exploited by the opponent.

Goalkeepers should have all the skills of all other field players but must also concentrate most completely on their own unique set of techniques necessary to play in the goal. These techniques are:

1.) Positioning
2.) Catching the ball
3.) Punching the ball

4.) Diving to the ball
5.) Throwing the ball
6.) Kicking

Goalkeeper Positioning
Body
Goalkeepers need to be able to react instantaneously. The body must be balanced and weight equally distributed on both feet, with knees slightly bent in a crouched position, hands half up and half down and the eyes fixed on the ball.

In relation to the goal
The goalkeeper must assume the most central position possible to ensure the greatest chance of being able to save the ball if it goes toward the goal. A thorough understanding of angles and your abilities (how far and fast can you react) is necessary.

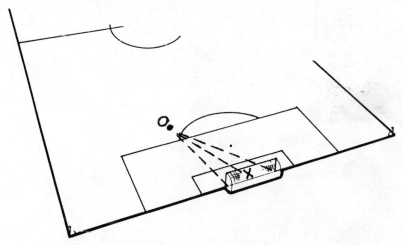

When a goalkeeper changes his angle to the ball it is important to keep the center of gravity low so you can move quickly if the opponent suddenly shoots. Goals should never be scored to the near post. The goalkeeper must cut that option off and force the shot to the far post, where the attacker's percentage of accuracy is reduced.

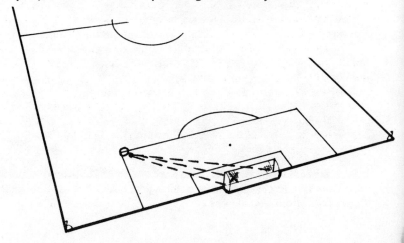

Catching the ball

The golden rule is to always have two body parts behind the ball. The goalkeeper catches the ball in his hands but has his chest or legs behind the ball in case he mishandles the first attempt. When catching the ball get the thumbs behind the ball and spread the fingers to form a large, wide, secure web. When you catch the ball this web should cushion or kill the momentum of the shot, making it easier to handle.

Goalkeepers must concentrate on watching the ball all the way through to conclusion. Errors result from carelessness.

Sometimes it's not possible to catch or punch the ball, and it must be safely played over the bar and out of play.

Punching the ball

When you cannot catch the ball it may be necessary to clear the ball over attackers and defenders with an explosive punch with the fist. Remember, this is only a last resort. Catch whenever you can. Punch only when it is necessary for safety first.

When punching is going to be necessary gauge the approach, leap forward and up, extend both arms, close both hands to provide the largest, flatest surface possible with your knuckles and punch through the ball. You must master two-handed as well as one-handed punches. Two-handed is preferred because it increases the odds of success. Punch for height, distance, and width. These factors will give your defense time to organize.

Punch for

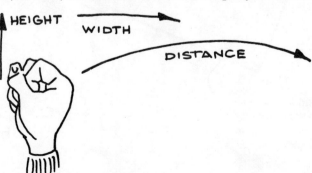

HEIGHT WIDTH DISTANCE

39

Diving to the ball

Dive only when necessary. Diving can be necessary because of poor positioning by the goalkeeper or a result of a well placed shot— or BOTH. Diving is spectacular. Good diving technique will decrease the risk of injury and increase the chances of making the save. Increasing the reaction speed and by getting the early jump on the ball will be helpful in saving the impossible shots. From the basic position the cross-over step is most common in making the diving save. If the ball is within reach save it with the hands. If unable to catch the ball turn it around the posts with a flick of the hands.

Pictures   High
                      Medium
                      Low
                      Flick over around the posts

Throwing the ball

A goalkeeper must be able to dispose of the ball quickly once he receives it. Whatever style a goalkeeper uses it must be done accurately and without hesitation.

Kicking - Goalkeepers

All goalkeepers must be able to clear the ball by punting from his hands, dead balls from goal kicks or restarts within his penalty area. Don't accept it until your GK has mastered all of these facets of his game.

Pressure Training Goalkeeper

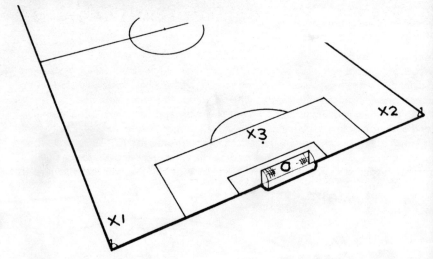

High ball from #1 - save it
Low Ball from #3 - Save it
High ball from #2 - Save it
Low ball from #3 - Save it

Alternating sides
High   Low

40

Brazil vs. England in Los Angeles, 1976. The Brazilian goalkeeper has been caught out of position, as the cross came from his left. The near post is not protected.

The Aztecs are on the attack, and the ball is in the penalty area. # 4 is leaving his defensive assignment. What tactical options are open to the Aztec players?

CHAPTER THREE

SYSTEMS AND TACTICS

SYSTEMS AND TACTICS

Systems of Play

The way in which eleven players will be organized on the field will be defined by fans and media as your system. Far too much interest and emphasis is placed on "finding the right system". No system will overcome bad technique, lack of effort, concentration, good judgement, individual and team cooperation, and basic intelligence. We can therefore conclude that systems do not win games— good players, effective tactics, and proper execution do! As the game of soccer changed, so did the popular systems of play. An accurate historical capsule of systems would include the following:

(1) Prior to 1925— most teams deployed 2 fullbacks, 3 halfbacks, and 5 forwards (two wings, two inside forwards and a center forward).

(2) After 1925— "W-M" formation was caused by a change in the offside law, reducing from 3 to 2 the number of opponents required between attacking players and their goal line.

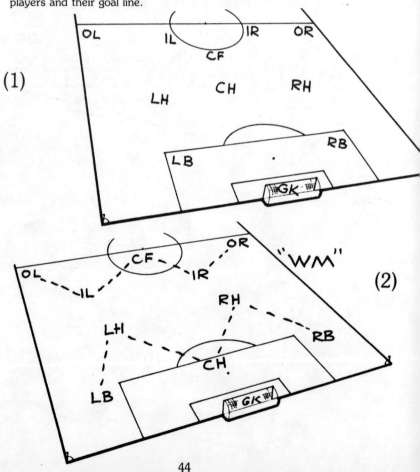

In the "WM" system the center half withdrew to a purely defensive role covering both fullbacks, and the two inside forwards withdrew to help control the midfield. Wing play was essential, with strong emphasis on a stalwart, opportunistic centerforward.

Adjustments would be made to the "WM" to make it suit individual team problems and preferences, withdrawing the right or left half into a defensive role. This made the "WM" appear to be a more modern 4-2-4. However that was to come!

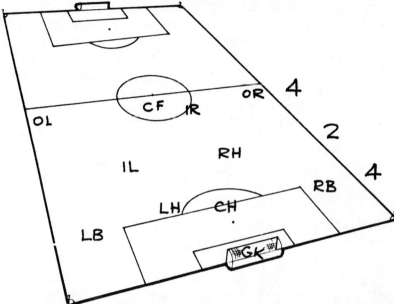

All coaches had to look at the "WM" and try to exploit the weaknesses of the system. So came the

(3) Deep Center Forward

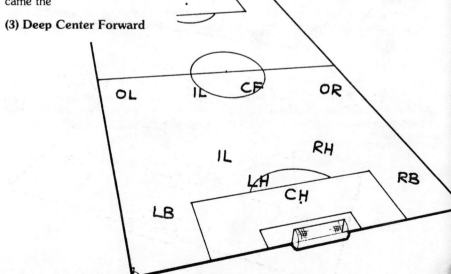

If the CF is withdrawn to midfield and the two insides are pushed forward we now find the CH exposed by two players.

It looked like this:

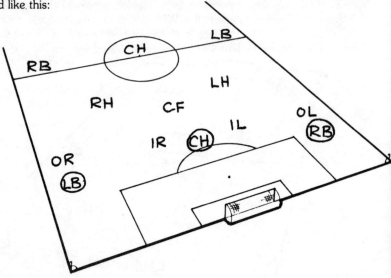

This system relied upon intelligent running off the ball by the inside forwards, in an attempt to lure the CH into false positions exposing space behind or in front of him for the ball to be played.

Any system is easy to play against if it is so rigid that it does not allow individual players to improvise and utilize their skill. So it was with the "WM" — teams tried to exploit the inherent weakness.

(4) 4-2-4 System

The 4-2-4 deploys a double CH concept in defense. It places tremendous burden on the two halfbacks or *linkmen*. The basic concept also has structured a team to have at least 6 players in attack when they have the ball and at least seven players in defense when they don't have possession. In the 1958 World Cup, won by Brazil, there were 126 goals scored in 35 games.

The Brazilians were the masters of the 4-2-4 and this system was felt to exemplify all that was good in attacking soccer. When teams are scoring lots of goals, good opposing coaches must think of ways to stop them from scoring. This is what happened: In the World Cup in 1962 there were only 88 goals scored in 32 games — 38 fewer goals — and a decrease of nearly 25%. Teams all over the world began deploying more and more players into defensive positions. Sweepers, defensive midfielders, 8 and 9 defenders became commonplace in world class teams. This type of soccer was so negative that games became stalemates. Teams were not willing to go forward and create chances to score. 0-0 became the slogan of the era. If you scored, you surely won 1-0. This type of play was exemplified by the

(5) Sweeper System

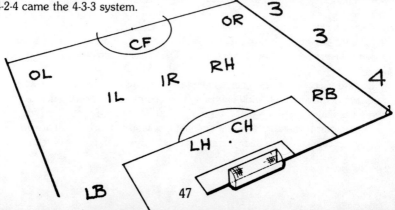

Where the CH covered 4 FB's, a defensive midfield player, and all 4 front players retreated behind the ball in defense! Nothing could be more negative.

(6) 4-3-3 System

In 1966 England won the World Cup utilizing players possessing tremendous work rates with a high level of tactical understanding within the team. In 90 minutes the ball is in play 60 minutes. Assuming that each team had the ball 30 minutes, each player has less than 3 minutes to perform with the ball. Even this figure is exaggerated, for the ball is between players (in the air or on the ground) at least 40% of the time. For 57 minutes each player must work hard to stop opponents and make it easier for their teammates when they are in possession. Therefore, *work without the ball will guarantee success.* Thus evolving from the 4-2-4 came the 4-3-3 system.

47

Tactics

The 4-3-3 provided more defensive balance in midfield than the 4-2-4 and also allowed a more sturdy base to build attacks from the midfield.

The 4-3-3 became widely used and accepted throughout the 1960's and is still the most popular system today.

However, in 1970 in Mexico in the World Cup Brazil again was to win the championship utilizing the 4-2-4 system of all-out attack. They could afford to do so with their imaginative attacking players like Pele, and Rivelino, and Tostao. The world marvelled at their skill, speed, and seemingly unending imagination and offensive coordination. In 1974 the national team of Holland (and to a lesser extent West Germany) was to unveil *Total Soccer* in which all ten field players were given less rigid functions and greater range to operate and improvise, with Johann Cruyff as their central figure.

Finally, in 1978 host country Argentina won a convincing overtime victory by defeating Holland. The emotions of the final eliminations once again brought attacking soccer, but no dominating personalities were evident. It is possible that in a short while not even the soccer enthusiasts will be able to name the players in this competition. Throughout history, the great personalities are what has made the game great. Sadly, the hard demands of the game may well be discouraging the full development of the individual. It is beginning to show on the field, and in the financial reports of clubs around the world.

The demands of play in modern soccer are awesome. Systems should exploit your strengths and disguise your weaknesses. Games are lost, not because of a system but because of a downfall in a specific area of team play such as poor shooting or poor defensive marking of opponents. The players you have will dictate the system and style your team will play. The important concept that you must understand and appreciate is that in working with basic formations (systems), players must be conditioned to move into basic positions at the right time. Simplicity is genius in team play and in the understanding of systems. All players in all teams must be able to find time and space in order to play at top efficiency. Today the American style of play is too methodical and slow in preparation of the ball for play in the game.

Charles Hughes, a well-known English F.A. coach, makes a basic assumption regarding positioning of players in modern soccer today as follows:

> We need at least four defenders . . .
> We need at least two midfielders . . .
> We need at least two forwards . . .
> We need a goalkeeper . . .

So, all we have left to decide is where we will utilize two players. Where can the two remaining players best suit our team tactics? This is a decision that you, the coach, must make.

In the modern concept of soccer, systems of play are directly related to tactics. Simply stated, tactics are anything and everything that you can do in preparation of your team for the immediate opponent— short term planning. Tactics are contrasted with *strategy*, which is long term planning of your team over a season or more. What are you going to do with your college team which is starting 8 of 11 freshmen on the varsity? What if in youth soccer you have seven players of 15 that have never played before and you start play in two weeks? These are real problems that you must solve and develop your plans within your limitations and up to your potential. This in fact is part of the S.A.I.D. Principle.— Specific Adaptations for Imposed Demands— conditioning of the mind and body to the conditions of the game. To do this properly we must have a complete knowledge and theoretical understanding of the three basic principle phases of play in the game. These are attack, defense, and midfield play. General tactics in attack include running into space (mobility), playing without the ball, combination play (providing width, depth, and penetration to your team), dribbling (improvisation) and finally scoring (goal-shot finishing).

General tactics in defense include immediate chase by all players, falling back and delaying the opponent, man to man marking (requiring concentration and balance within the team), zone defense (providing cover), and finally the man and the ball— dispossessing him and counterattack. The counterattack has as its basic principles:

(1) Push into open space.
(2) Pass into open space.
(3) Follow the ball. Take short cuts.
(4) Dribble self-confidently.
(5) Use wall passing.
(6) Use centering and score.

General tactics in midfield play include keeping the ball (maintaining possession), changing the speed and direction of the game, using the ball and space intelligently, and most importantly going through and having confidence to score goals.

These general tactics must be understood by your players. Your players must possess an understanding of theoretical terms so you can efficiently and effectively discuss the game with them. In relation to tactics the field is divided into three basic parts: defensive third, middle third, and the attacking third. The position of the ball establishes where these parts are at various times in the game. We can use these terms when we discuss tactics before, during and after games so that we can easily identify a general area of play to point out strengths or weaknesses. Some useful terms we should incorporate are:

Destructive Soccer - In the modern concept, where all ten field players try to win the ball in defense and
Attacking Soccer - Where all ten field players are involved in offensive movements with and without the ball.

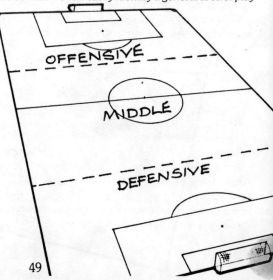

We must teach players to do this. Be fluid. Be there. Players must be willing to sacrifice for the benefit of the team (psychology). Players must be able to recognize what is developing before it happens (intelligence). In fluid play, training for movement without the ball must be conditioned and explained.

Example:

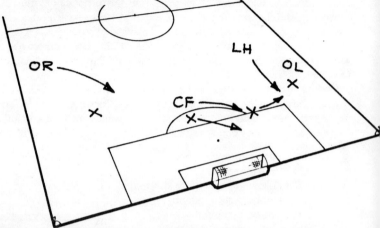

In the *Attacking Third* OL has the ball. The OR must understand that staying wide is important. Have patience. Time his run in combination with movement of CF and possibly LH. When LH and CF run, both cover defenders are cleared from the space for OR to run into and receive the ball.

Defensive tactics in modern soccer must include an understanding for low pressure (where all defenders simply retreat behind the ball and wait for the attack) and high pressure (which is characterized by close man-to-man marking all over the field).

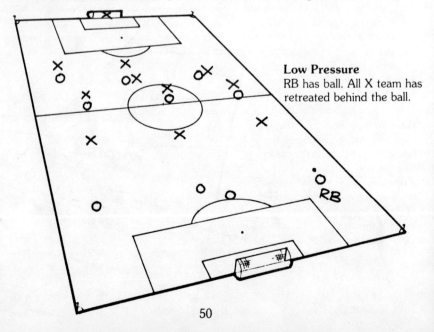

Low Pressure
RB has ball. All X team has retreated behind the ball.

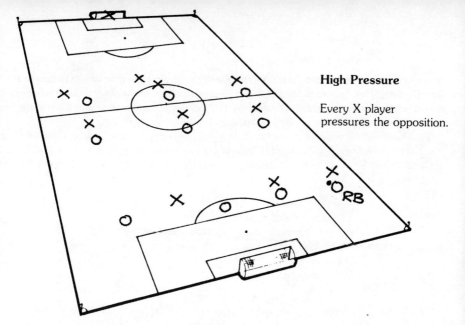

Every X player
pressures the opposition.

Each player must understand his teammates' action in order to apply pressure in any division of the field during a game. What basic positions will all players assume at a given time?

Example:

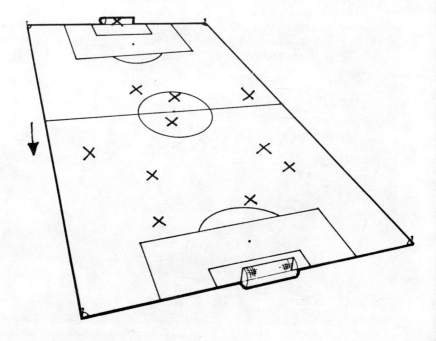

51

When team X loses the ball in the attacking third will they play low pressure in their attacking third or high pressure? If two players play high pressure and the others do not, their efforts will be wasted. Or will they play low pressure and retreat to the halfway line and then pick up man to man or zone marking?

The tactics of your team must be developed through a series of drills—or repetitions. These repetitions must occur (1) with no pressure, (walking) the (2) low pressure (half speed) and finally (3) high pressure (game conditions). Your tactics will be affected by the following:

    (1)   The level of skill in your team
    (2)   The level of skill of your opponent and the
    (3)   circumstances (injuries, weather, intelligence).

We must subidivide tactics into the following three categories:

    (1)   individual
    (2)   group and
    (3)   team.

Each category must be given special attention.

Sometimes players' tactics involve violent play or other forms of misconduct. Referees and coaches should be equally strong in their condemnation of these tactics.

The correct shoulder charge is both a tactic and a skill.

INDIVIDUAL TACTICS

   Winning individual battles all over the field will go a long way towards determining the team's success or failure. Individual tactics include everything that is required to keep possession of the ball for your team. The classic battle of 1 versus 1 and the development of a fighting spirit is a top priority. Working without the ball, dribbling, passing, shooting, and tackling, are all included in individual tactics.

Exercises Individual tactics   1 versus 1

1) In twos
   Dribbling and screening partner from getting the ball
   30-60 second intervals

2) In threes
   Two are dribbling and one rests — the man who loses possession of the ball will rest as the free man tackles
   10 yards x 10 yards area

3) Two pairs — interval training   2 yard square

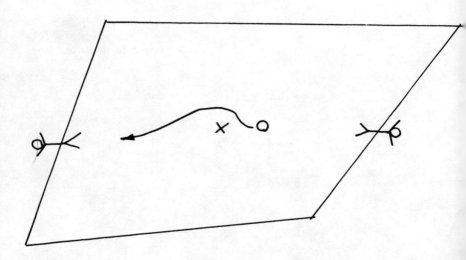

1st pair dribbles to score goals. Goals scored by pushing ball through legs of resting pair. One or two minutes.

4) From end line to half-field line

X tries to cross half way line without O still being in front of him, by feinting and bluffing. Change speed and direction quickly.

5) 1 versus 1   30 yards square   Interval style
   2 large goals   2 goalkeepers   1-3 minutes

1 versus 1 with goal shots. GK save — give to teammate, and attack.

6) 1 versus 1   20 yards square   Plus neutral GK

Attack from either side of goal.

7) Functional training for fullbacks
   2 Fullbacks in pairs

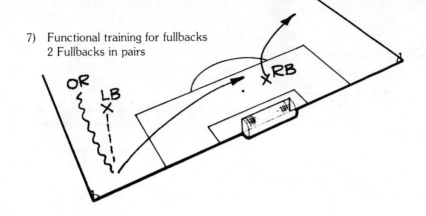

LB jockeys OR along sideline into corner and tackles if possible. OR tries to center ball and RB clears.

8) Functional training of wings

9) Winger versus Fullback (1 versus 1)

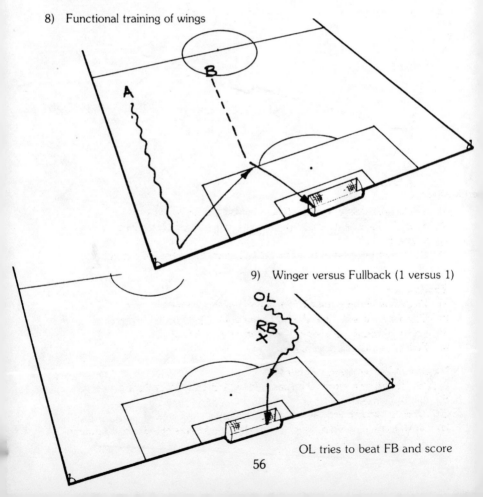

OL tries to beat FB and score

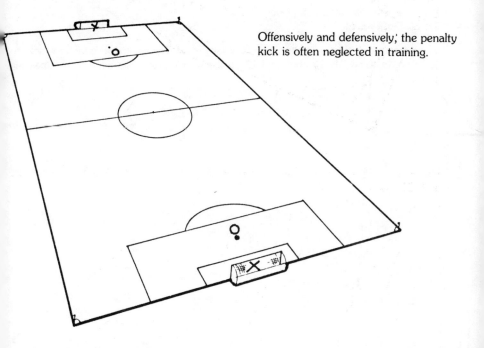

Offensively and defensively, the penalty kick is often neglected in training.

e Goalkeeper

1) Try to break kicker's concentration by subtle delaying tactics.
2) Read the kicker's approach (If you have not scouted his tendencies) — watch only the ball!
3) React. Extend yourself and flick the ball around the post if it can not be caught.

The Kicker

1) Place ball on spot yourself, making sure it is perfect
2) Choose your side, and don't change your mind.
3) Follow through your kick. Have authority
4) Follow up, in case it is blocked.

Functional Training of centerback
A) Serve low balls from all angles— Have CB clear to target players.
B) Serve high balls
C) Various service with attackers to challenge.
D) With extra defenders, push out and pull attackers offside on command.

Goalkeeper Tactics

Factors:
A. Positioning
B. Cooperation with back players
1st player in attack

1) 6 versus 6, with one small goal and one large goal. Team with GK counterattacks to small goal with no GK. Use half field. Use this game to set up walls, corners, backpassing to GK.

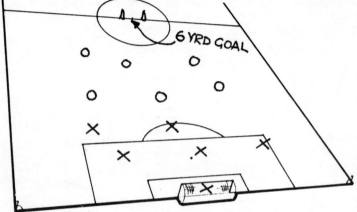

2) Serve balls to GK — high, low, medium — alternating

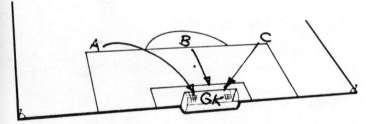

3) Goal shots from an angle, for positioning

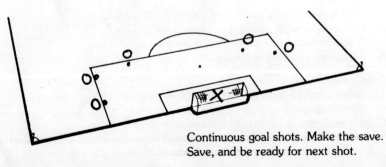

Continuous goal shots. Make the save. Save, and be ready for next shot.

58

4) Distribution — GK first link in attacking movement. Note: can be done at alternating speed.

5) Goalkeepers
Goalkeeper throws to X^1 who lst times to X^2 who first times cross to X^3. No opposition.

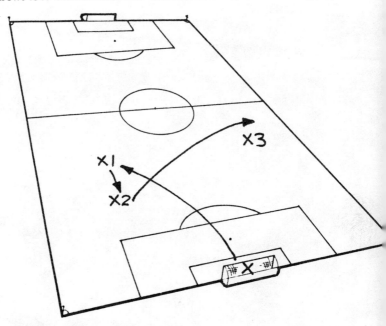

6) Goalkeeper — attacking tactics

Throwing
1. Switching play is important
2. Quality, speed, and accuracy, for keeping possession.

Kicking
1. Fast release when possible.
2. Stretch opposition end to end on field.
3. Play secondary possession (gain control of rebound from defender)

Goal Kick
1. Quality — long or short, just like a pass.
2. Speed — to gain numerical advantage.
3. Short. To keep possession.

(Should be responsibility of Goalkeeper)

59

The moulding of individual players into a group may be the coach's biggest challenge.

GROUP TACTICS

When two or more players (up to 8 versus 8) are involved in coordinated attack or defense their actions are referred to as group tactics. Numerical superiority is required around the ball. You must have more attackers than they have defenders and more defenders than they have attackers.

Exercises are necessary to develop effective interplay among teammates, such as the changing positions, knowing the defensive roles of wings and halfbacks, the coordination of goalkeeper and defenders, and forwards and midfielders.

Exercises Group tactics

1)   2 versus 1

10 yards in square area
A)   Player without ball must find open space and run into it.
B)   Wall passes — second player comes close to set it up.
C)   1 touch — possession soccer. (extremely difficult) shooting at goal

2)   2 versus 1

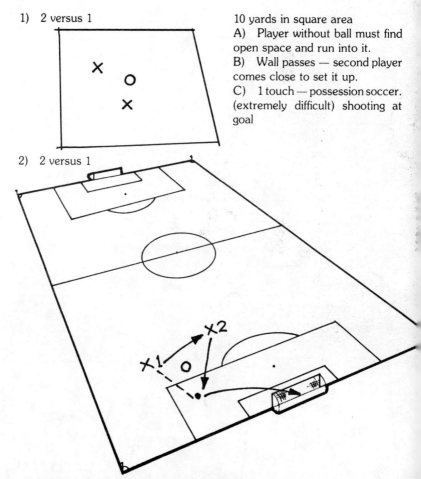

Square pass X¹ - X² run for double pass and shot on goal.

61

3) 3 versus 1

10 yard area, Interval style (30 - 60 sec.)

a) with dribbling until pressured
b) two-touch

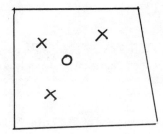

4) 4 versus 2
1 touch for the X's

small goal O's def.
large goal X's def.
20 yards square
O's may counterattack, and shoot
from any distance.

6FT GOAL

12 FT GOAL

5) 2 versus 2

Carrying the ball in hands. 30 yards square. No goals. Player in possession is tagged — other team takes over. Teaches feinting, and running to open space.

6) 2 versus 2   20 yards square   Intervals 1 - 2 minutes

to one common goal   to two goals   to three goals

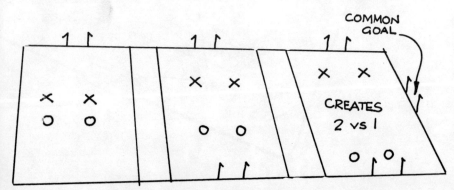

COMMON GOAL

CREATES
2 vs 1

7) 5 versus 5   40 yards square

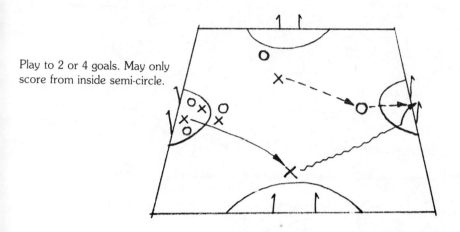

Play to 2 or 4 goals. May only
score from inside semi-circle.

8) 3 versus 3   30 yards square   Interval method   1-5 minutes

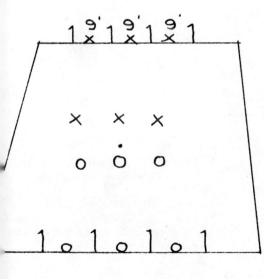

Playing to 3 goals versus 3
GK's, who may not use hands.

Variations: Use 2 GK's who
protect the 3 goals.

Balls may be shot head-height.

9) 3 versus 3 30 yards square 15 yards x 10 yards neutral space, where no player may enter to shoot.

1 yard goal

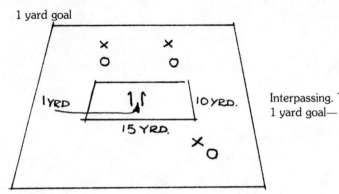

Interpassing. Try to score through 1 yard goal— continuously

10) 4 versus 4 40 square yards 5 minutes. Interval method to 4 goals

Large goals

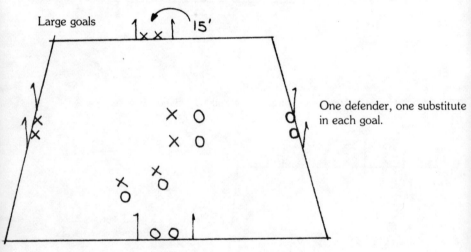

One defender, one substitute in each goal.

11) 1 versus 2 with playmaker

O[1] must free himself for pass from O and get shot on goal.
No GK
Variations: Other combinations, 2 versus 3, 3 versus 4, etc. Work against the odds
Remember: Success here is just the shot on goal.

12) 3 versus 4   1 goal against sweeper

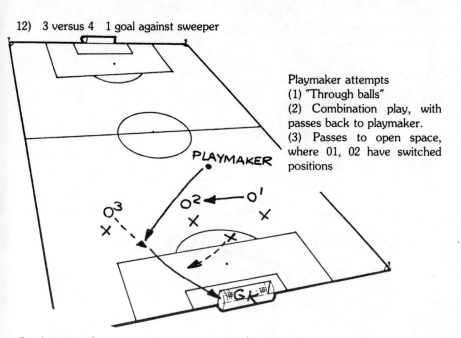

Playmaker attempts
(1) "Through balls"
(2) Combination play, with passes back to playmaker.
(3) Passes to open space, where 01, 02 have switched positions

Combination play to expose sweeper — rapid interpassing

13) 2 versus 1   Wing play

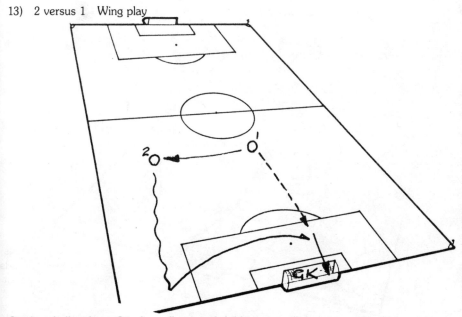

O^1 plays ball wide to O^2 who collects and dribbles to endline cross — for O^1 to score versus X and GK

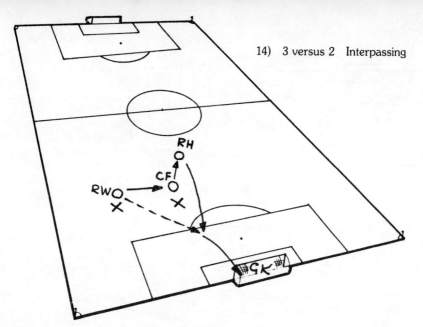

14) 3 versus 2 Interpassing

RW square pass CF. Back pass to RH. RW runs recives chip pass from RH. Goal shot.

15) 3 versus 1

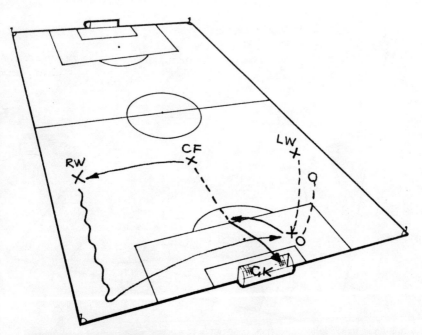

CF square pass to right wing
RW dribbles to end line, centering cross to LW who heads back to CF for shot on goal
Try first without opponent, to ensure success and build confidence.

16) In threes
Straight passes — zigzag running length of field — finish with 18 yard goal shot.

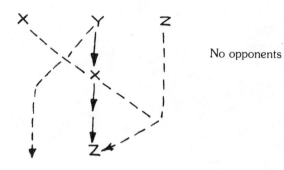

No opponents

17) 3 versus 1 in 10 yard square

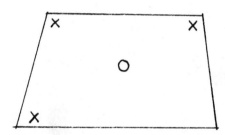

1 touch — count consecutive number of passes — player making bad pass comes in.

Movement: support angles to receive pass
Variable conditions: inside left foot only/left or right foot only/outside foot only

18) 4 versus 2   20 yards square

Conditions — 1 touch. 2 touch if too difficult. Count only through passes (those which intersect the 2 defenders)

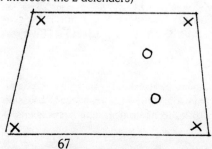

19) 4 versus 4   4 in thirds of the field

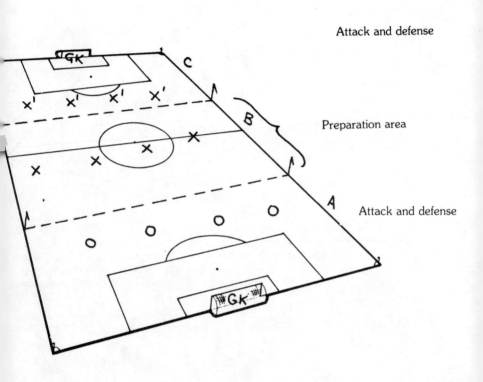

Attack and defense

Preparation area

Attack and defense

X's attack O's — 4 versus 4 in A zone — X's try to score if O's win ball X's try to regain possession before O's leave zone A. O's must dribble, or control — pass ball out of zone A to zone B. In zone B, the O's regroup 1 touch interpassing and prepare to attack X's in other end. Repeat.

Emphasis on:
    (1)   Ability of attacking team to score goals.
    (2)   Immediate pressure to regain possession in attacking third
    (3)   Ability to make transition from defense to attack.

20) 3 versus 3   Counter attack   Half or full field

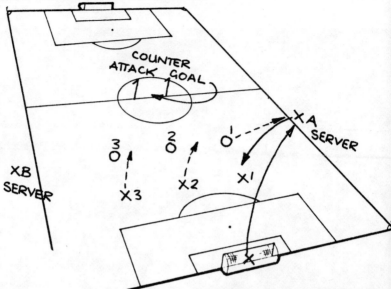

X's and O's 1, 2, 3 play 3 versus 3 to large goal. When X GK receives ball he immediately throws ball to server XA or XB. Immediate pressure is placed on server XA by O^1. The server passes ball to attackers (X's) as soon as O^1 has committed himself. They play counterattack 3 versus 2 utilizing numerical superiority in which you attack with the ball and commit defenders. (When your team has numerical disadvantage in attack you attack without the ball.)

Once O has committed himself, he must remain out of play for 15 seconds. If a goal has not been scored, server and O, both join play, creating a new advantage for Team X.

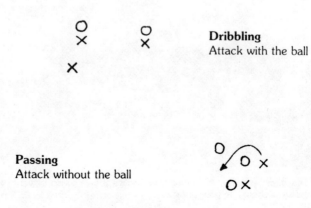

Dribbling
Attack with the ball

Passing
Attack without the ball

There's not too much you can do about team tactics if you coach players "under 14." The development of skills should be your priority.

TEAM TACTICS

The successful play of all eleven members of the team requires great team understanding. Development of this understanding begins with numerical situations from half games 6 versus 5 to 11 versus 11. Team tactics incorporate all individual and group tactics. It is in effect the composite of everyone's actions on the field of play. The idea in training for team tactics is to simulate highly realistic game situations and emphasize specific aspects of individual and collective play, pointing out their inter-relationships.

Exercises   Team Tactics
1)   From the kickoff:

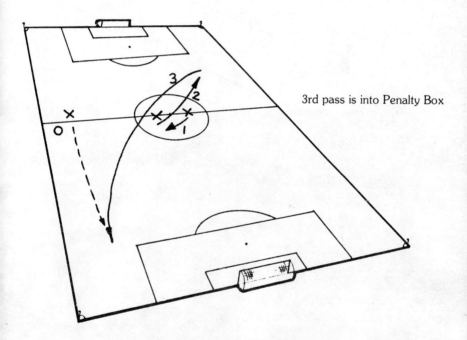

3rd pass is into Penalty Box

A kickoff, just as any set play, can be rehearsed, and can catch the opposition by surprise!

2) 11 versus 11 Full field

Play full game *across* the field to 2 goals — all players (except GK) must be in attacking half to score.

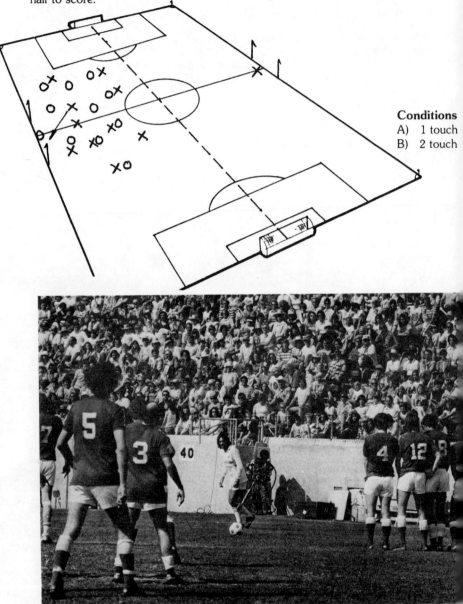

Conditions
A) 1 touch
B) 2 touch

The setting up of walls on free kicks is sometimes effective. The taking of kicks, however, often comes as a surprise even to the attacking team!

3) Setting up defensive walls

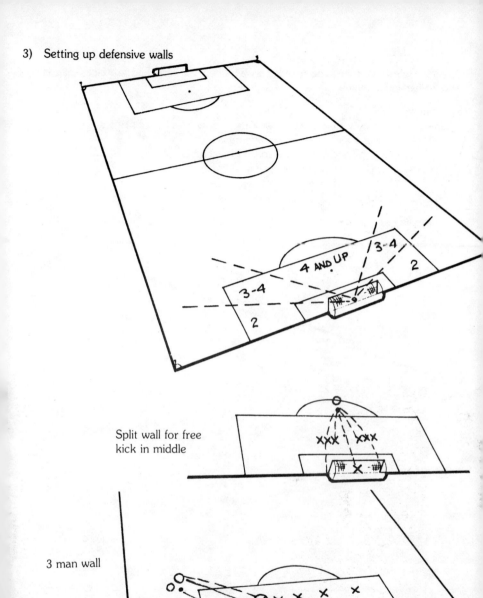

Split wall for free kick in middle

3 man wall

Wall covers space on near post. GK covers far half of goal. Man on near post of wall sets it up. Wall should be tight — no balls go through the wall — shoulder to shoulder. Only give as much reasonable distance from the ball as Referee demands. Additional players mark vital space, and have the most important job.

73

*Indirect kick — 4th man added to edge of wall; when ball is touched he attacks the ball— and 3 man wall remains intact.

Keys in defense
1) Set the wall up quickly with the proper number of players
2) Prevent kick from being taken quickly
3) Occupy additional vital space on each side of wall
4) Goalkeeper in proper position
5) Be alert and react decisively
6) No walls needed onkicks from legal 35 yards.

4) Free kicks in attack

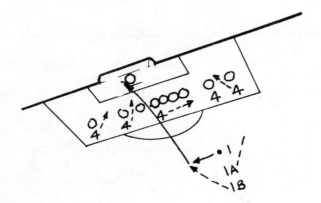

In this case 1 pushes for 1B from altered angle — through cleared space. 1A makes deceptive run to right.

Either player may strike ball, push it square, chip it, or lift it.

Free kick ideas. A pass to the wall.

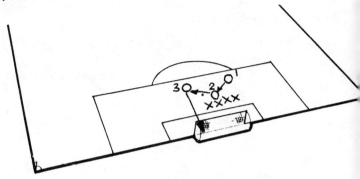

O^1 pass to O^2 in wall — back to O^3 who has an angle at goal clear of the wall.

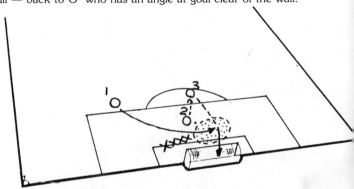

O^2 and O^3 exchange places and O^1 chips ball to space

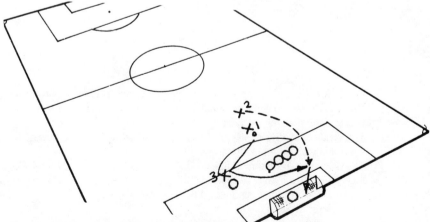

X^2 runs past ball — X^1 passes to X^3 who passes around wall to X^2.

Key Points for Free Kicks

    1) Have most intelligent and skillful users of ball at the ball. They must evaluate prospects for success.

    2) Deception is key to success. Movement is imperative.

    3) Powerful, swerving shots that are accurate cause great problems for the defense, but few players are capable of executing them.

    4) *Attacking Players* should occupy defending players — make them have a job instead of standing free to cover.

    5) Add players to the defensive wall.

    6) Follow up all shots.

    7) Use at least 3 variations.

5) Defense at corner kick

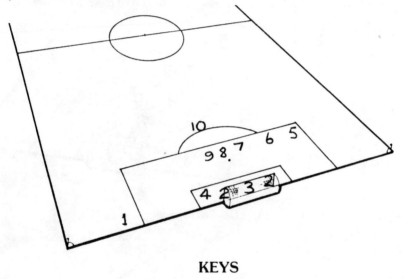

KEYS

    1) Protect against short corner

    2) Defenders on each post. Near post player attacks ball— both cover goal line if GK leaves to catch or punch ball. (Some goalkeepers prefer not to have a player defend at the far post.)

    3) Position of GK is slightly towards back post. Own the 6 yard box, as everything in there belongs to you.

    4) Occupies space and attacks ball. Cuts out low-driven balls. 5-6-7-8-9-10 — Pick up man to man tight marking of opponents. Get to the ball first and clear for height, width, and distance. When kick is cleared rush out of penalty area for counter attack.

6) Attack at corner kicks

KEYS

1-2)   Fake or take short corner — numerical superiority. Second attacking player will draw another defensive player. This may open a space near the goal.
3)   Long corner to a heading specialist. Head for goal or deflect ball down for players following.
4)   Occupy defenders.
5)   Movement, attacking the ball. Coordination between kick and movements is important.

7)   Defending at throw-ins

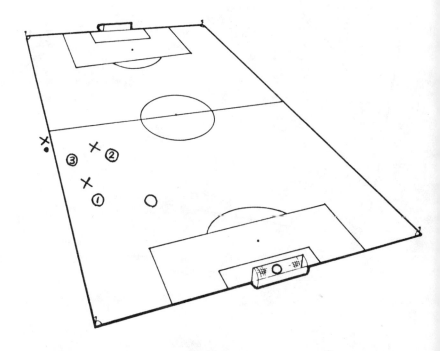

KEYS

A)   1-2-3 mark thrower and have an extra defender in the area of the throw.
B)   Pressurize the control of the throw. Try to win possession.
C)   •Concentrate. Teams have a tendency to relax and expose themselves when the ball is dead.
D)   Defending against long throws in attacking third — treat them as a corner kick!!!!

8) Attacking at throw-ins

KEYS:

A)   Get ball in play quickly to an open man in a forward position.
B)   Make it a simple throw that is easy to control.
C)   Create movement around the throw to create space.
D)   Keep possession of the ball.
E)   Get thrower back in the game because he will often be unmarked

Examples — Keep it simple

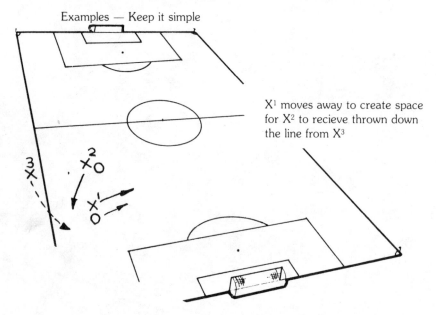

X^1 moves away to create space for X^2 to recieve thrown down the line from X^3

Attacking with long throw in attacking third

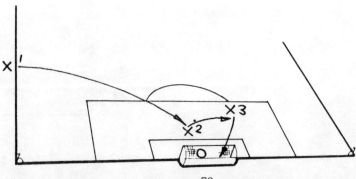

9) Corner Kick Ideas

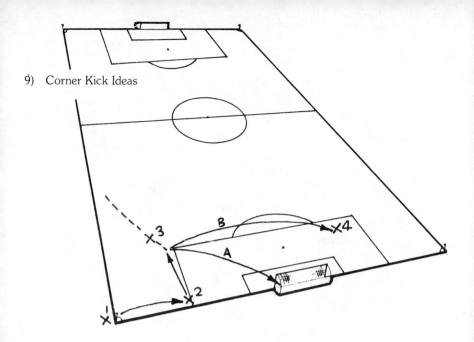

X^1 to X^2 to X^3 who has run from deep position: Shoot (A) or chip against far post (B)

Another corner kick

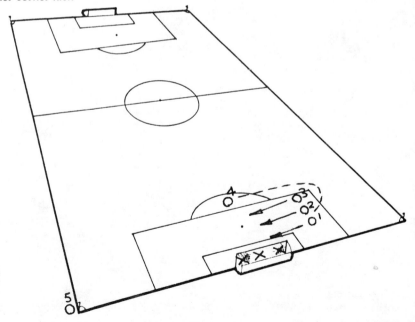

O 1-2-3 run diagonally   O4 circles behind to collect a slightly delayed kick.

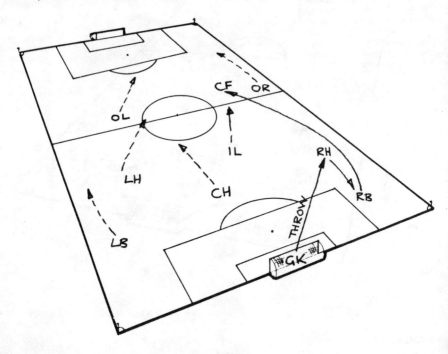

GK throws to RH — knocks back to RB who hits ball to CF who can control or flick to OR, IL, OL

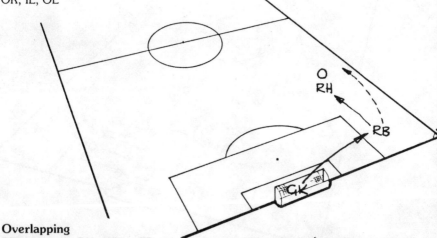

Overlapping
RB runs past RH. When FB runs he must recieve the ball. Intelligent running is important.

Your methods in attack will culminate in serious attempts on goal.

Kicking at goal seldom pays off. The practice of shooting at goal under game conditions brings succe

CHAPTER FOUR

THE BACK OF THE NET

THE BACK OF THE NET

"Everyone wants to score, but no one knows how goals are scored..."

—A Famous Coach
(Reprinted without permission)

A successful youth coach taught his players to "pass to the back of the net." He didn't start out that way, thinking at first that scoring would be easy, and desired, by players. It can become discouraging for you, as you witness the breakdown in accuracy, authority, and concentration when players go near the goal. Basketball, a sport which is sometimes compared with soccer, encourages scoring, for few players want to play defense. Soccer, on the other hand, develops defensive systems first, scorers last.

Each goal for and against you should reveal multitudes about your team. You and your players should be able to dissect each goal, whether it is scored for or against your team.

All goals occur from combinations of the following: unmarked attacking players, attacking players who have beaten an isolated defender, lack of pressure on the ball, and finally lack of organization during set pieces.

To score goals we must understand the above circumstances and place strong emphasis on shooting. "Finishing" is perhaps the most undercoached aspect of soccer in the United States. Finding goal scorers anywhere is a difficult task. When you find one — keep him, for there is one for every 10 defenders. We must develop scorers who are composed under pressure, who understand the value of accurate powerful shooting and who are skillful enough to create scoring chances for themselves. They must also be opportunistic enough to see goal scoring chances when they occur.

GOAL SHOOTING

In Stationary Position
    A)   Dead balls — 18-30 yds. From all reasonable angles.
    B)   Half-volley.

2 Players
    Wall Pass — one touch control and shoot
    Wall Pass - shoot 1st time

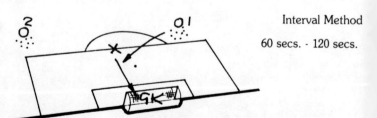

Interval Method

60 secs. - 120 secs.

Service from O¹ and O² alternating X control ball 1 touch and shoot. 2nd touch immediate control and quick shot.

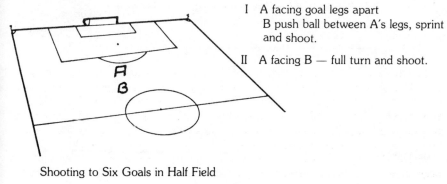

I   A facing goal legs apart
    B push ball between A's legs, sprint
    and shoot.

II A facing B — full turn and shoot.

Shooting to Six Goals in Half Field

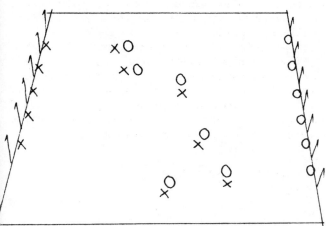

6 versus 6 in the middle, with one ball. When a goal is scored all goalkeepers change. Goalkeepers on line only, and may not use hands. Change if goal not scored in two minutes.

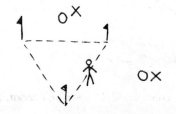

3 Flags Forming 3 Goals

2 versus 2 in 20 yds. square

Intense work for Goalkeeper.
Rapid shooting and training to get free and score goal quickly.

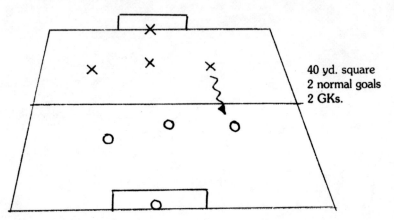

Shoot from within your own half — limit number to ability — GK roll ball out to teammate to start match. Players may not venture into opponent's half.

Combination Shooting

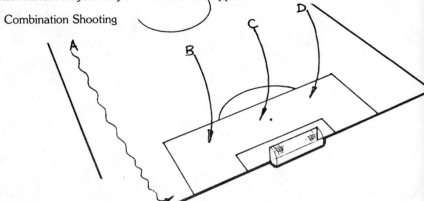

A winger dribbles top speed to end line.
B runs near post.
C runs central.
D runs far post.

Each working for the other. roles may be interchanged. Use crossing patterns.

Pressure Training

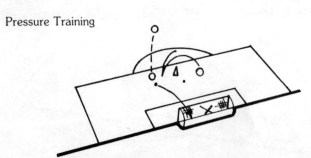

Marker at 16 yds. GK/shooter sprints right and left around marker and shoots from service alternating sides. Use specific number of balls (10-15) in prescribed period (30-60 seconds)

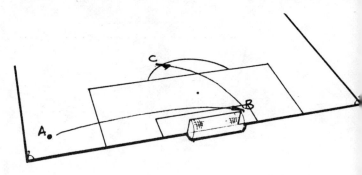

A cross to B, who heads down to C, who "times" first shot.

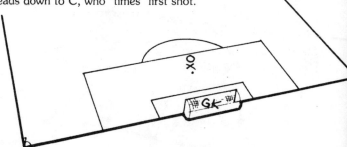

Service into goal area 1 versus 1. Get a shot in. Make space to shoot. Variation: Use two defenders.

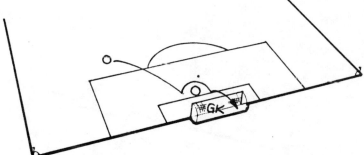

O — Balls served into box in air — 1st touch·control — 2nd touch Volley into goal.

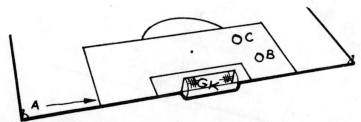

A dribbles along end line and serves ball to B or C (marked by defenders) at any time to score goals. Requires coordination of attackers, timing, and skill.

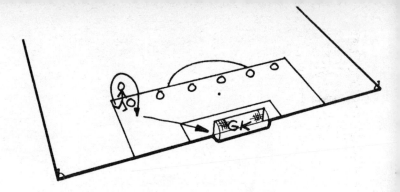

Player lifts ball with instep over head — turn — volley or half-volley into net.

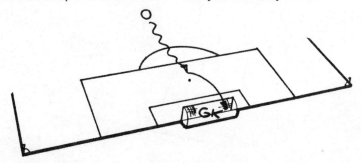

All angles. Run from mid-field, gradually accelerating. Shoot from 18 yards.

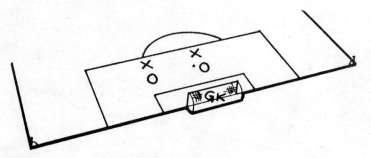

2 versus 2 to one goal inside 18 yd. box.

5 versus 5

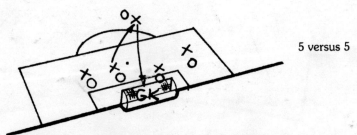

Goal can only be scored after being passed back out of penalty area.

Shooting practice pays off in a game.

Laurie Calloway stations himself between opponent and goal. Notice that eyes are on the ba[ll]

CHAPTER FIVE

KEEPING THEM FROM SCORING

KEEPING THEM FROM SCORING

In thinking defense, many coaches and players think of packed penalty areas, destructive, defensive tactics, and 0-0 games. The team which thinks defense continually is different, of course, from the team which thinks of defense as a key for obtaining an offensive thrust on goal. The quick transition from offense to defense occurs in the mind of a player in a millisecond, and is effective only if players work as a team.

Principles of Defensive Play

(1) Stay goal-side of the opponent.

(2) Support any teammate who needs it, trying constantly to gain a 2-1 numerical superiority.

(3) For "man-to-man" marking, stay close enough so the opponent's decisions have to be rushed.

(4) For "zone marking", cover the zone, and be prepared to sacrifice your space for others.

(5) Recognize that one or two successful, though short, passes means you've created an offense from a defense.

(6) Tackle only to win the ball. Otherwise, injury or loss of energy is risked.

Types of Defense

(1) Man-to-man, where strong, persevering players will prevail.

(2) Zone marking, where specified areas of the field are identified, usually in conformity with the strenths of the opponent. Great teamwork is required.

(3) A combination of (1) and (2), where a specific problem, such as a dominant opponent or a weak defensive teammate, occurs.

It is interesting to note that although defenses seem better organized than offenses, the negative, desperate calling between teammates most often occurs in the defense. Players cannot score as well as they can defend, and when the goal is allowed, it is usually a lapse in defense rather than a positive act of offense. If the desired discipline of the defense is attained, it will carry over to the offense, and more goals may result.

Defense

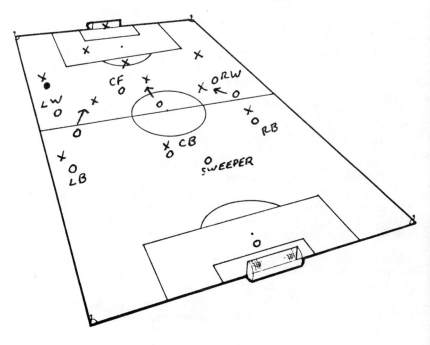

Low Pressure — in
attacking third
LW, CF, RW
Retreat, Mark Zones

LB, CB, RB
man to man
marking
sweeper — gives
cover

All must share equally in work — defense depends on consistent pressure

Defense

High Pressure —
immediately on
ball. Win it
back NOW!

One FREE man
farthest from ball in
negative area
LFB

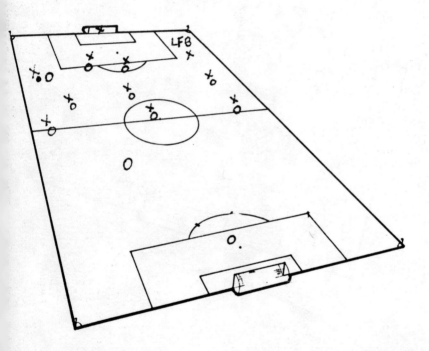

Pressure defense. U.S. vs. Mexico in a World Cup elimination game.

If you're not in shape, other members of the team will have to carry you.

CHAPTER SIX

PHYSICAL FITNESS

"Fatigue makes cowards of us all"

—Vince Lombardi

SOCCER PHYSICAL FITNESS

Many players say they are fit, fewer are, and fewer yet are willing to make the sacrifices necessary for fitness. General physical fitness is defined in many ways, but we need only concern ourselves with assessing the relative soccer fitness of our players. Everything is relative in the game, and the same is true of fitness. We must make our team as fit as possible to hope to achieve maxiumum efficiency in their performance. Every player has a potential level of fitness. The closer we get the player to that level, the better chance of success. Soccer fitness is deceivingly simple to profess yet extremely complicated to maintain and control. Athletes live individual lifestyles, and your fitness programs must accomodate such differences. Specialized programs at the college level and beyond must be developed to cope with the peculiarities of each individual athlete.

Fitness means that players can perform with maximum efficiency for the duration of the game, whether it be 80 minutes in high school, 90 minutes or more in college, senior amateur or professional soccer. Train players for the needs of the game. In the game they will need flexibility, endurance, speed, strength, agility, and mental toughness. These can all be conditioned and improved.

Flexibility (Stretching)

In 1975 we instituted a vigorous stretching program with our professional team. We practiced it religiously, and it worked. Stretching relaxes the player and readies the muscles for larger demands, and decreases the chances for injury. In the year when we instituted the stretching program, we experienced fewer pulled muscles in the hamstrings, thighs, and calves.

There are two types of stretching methods: *Dynamic* — bouncing or rocking while stretching and *Static*, without bouncing and rocking. Dynamic stretching is negative, for it accomplishes nothing and may prove harmful. There is a real risk of damaging muscles.

Static stretching positions must be held for 30-45 seconds without moving. This process over a period of time lengthens (stretches) body muscles. Hold the muscle position at a fine point just short of actual pain. You will be happy with the results. Stretch everyone, everyday, and with no exceptions.

Stretching before a heavy workout. Note the position of the player in the background. Each player stretches according to his own needs.

98

Endurance

Soccer players need a large endurance base for the demands of the game. Since a player may run 6-8 miles in a full game, great physiological reserve must be present. Most physiologists have agreed that endurance is composed of two phases:

PHASE ONE: Cardiovascular (the circulatory system takes oxygen to and removes waste products from the muscles).

PHASE TWO: Muscular.

Development of these two systems is most often accomplished by utilizing the overload principle, which is simply doing more than before ina planned, progressive manner. This principle utilizes the 3 R's — rate, resistance, and repetition. When we manipulate these three factors we have the potential to alter the effects of the training being accomplished. In essence for any given exercise we can a) increase the number of repetitions, b) increase the speed of the repetitions, c) increase the length of the repetitions, d) decrease the rest period between repetitions or e) increase the resistance, or work load.

Phase One - Cardiovascular: Endurance training is also either aerobic (the body has sufficient oxygen supply) or anaerobic (without sufficient oxygen). In aerobic training the supply of oxygen is equal to the body's demand. The pulse rate of the heart is increased and there is relative stability and rhythmical work within the body. Aerobic training is generalized as quantitative work (how far will you run?). The body is capable of sustaining this type of work over a longer period of time. In anaerobic training the oxygen supply is less than the body's demand. This heart is forced to push out more blood per stroke — hence stroke volume is increased. Anaerobic training is maximal work that cannot be sustained and is categorized as quality work.

Common examples

Aerobic Training

Marathon-type running — continuous rhythmical exercise over long distances at a moderate pace and of moderate intensity.

Anaerobic Training

Sprinting — running short and moderate distances at a very fast rate with maximum intensity.

Phase 2 - Endurance — Local Muscle Training

The specific muscle groups of the body need to be conditioned for the demands of the match. Special attention and exercises must be given to the following areas:

1) Legs and hips
2) Arms and shoulders
3) Trunk in extension and flexion
4) General body movements

Interval Training

This training utilizes both anaerobic and aerobic principles during which periods of work are interspersed with periods of rest (recovery).

Example

Players sprint 40 yards dribbling ball at full speed, then walk back juggling the ball. Develops speed, skill and concentration.

Speed

Speed is a highly complex topic, the result of muscle coordination. Speed is called many things — quickness, reflexes, reaction. Whatever you call it, it can generally be improved 10% to 15%. The key is overcoming lack of physical speed with improved ball technique. Train for pure speed utilizing a clock (time) and specified distances.

Example

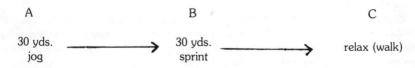

A   B   C

30 yds.   ⟶   30 yds.   ⟶   relax (walk)
jog   sprint

Distance and time — cover 30 yards in under 4 seconds (with competition of partner) jog-sprint-relax.

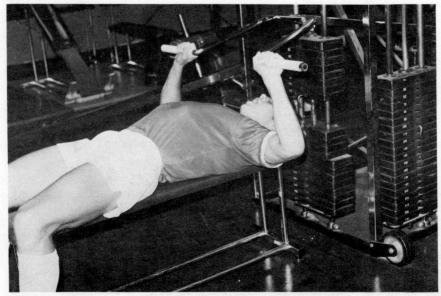

Weight training is important to a professional soccer player. Here is the famous "bench press." Sam Bick develops his chest area by pushing the weight to the full extension of the elbows.

Strength

Strength is the ability to overcome stable resistance, such as the resistance presented in a strong tackle. Soccer players need general body strength as well as extraordinary strength in their legs, abdomen, and arms to sustain a high level of performance.

Weight training can become negative if done so excessively that it restricts the fluid, supple movements necessary of the soccer player. Strength also helps to reduce the risk of injury to the athlete. Strength training usually falls into two categories — isometric and isotonic.

In isometric training (static) there is muscle contraction without the muscle actually shortening. No doubt you know how to engage in isometric training by simply pushing hard against the steering wheel of your car while driving. In isotonic training (dynamic) the muscle contracts with a shortening of the muscle fiber.

Examples
Isometric
Pushing against an unmovable object such as a brick wall.
Isotonic
Lifting weights through a full range of motion

Agility

Agility is the ability to change directions quickly with or without the ball. Great improvements can be made in a player's agility only as his fitness and skills are improved. Confidence to play quickly and to change direction instantly are important to your player's success.

Exercises

1) Obstacle course — with many jumps and turns. Specify times to complete course.
2) Dribbling through cones at top speed.
3) Interval training — 1 versus 1 in a small area — i.e. 20 yards square to small goals.

Good agility with 14-year-old players.

Mental Toughness

Mental toughness, known to all marathon runners, is the catchall phrase which is required to fight the various effects of fatigue. We train our players to become more physically prepared to delay the onset of fatigue. Fatigue causes the work rate of the athlete to decrease, his judgement to falter, the skill to deteriorate, and concentration is lost.

Regeneration

Regeneration is the time required for replacement of lost calories due to excessive physical activity. Growth (replacement) is the rebirth within the body after it has been torn down by activity.

Example - Fatigued athletes

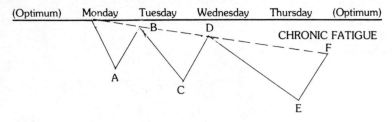

A- Play hard game.
B- Since end of Monday game, player has only returned to B, - which is still below Monday's starting point if training.
C- Result of hard training
D- Recovery below B
E- Result of hard training
F- Recovery below D

Regeneration may be accomplished in the following ways:

1) Sufficient time
2) Sleep and rest
3) Adequate nutrition (food)
4) Removal of fatigue products
5) Recreational activities

Rhythmic training program

Monday - light workout. Technique development. Review tactics from past game.
Tuesday - Heavy workout. Develop fitness and tactics.
Wednesday - Light workout. Technique development.
Thursday - Heavy workout. Develop tactics.
Friday - Light workout. Review tactics.
Saturday - GAME
Sunday - DAY OFF - TREATMENT OF INJURED

INTERVAL TRAINING CIRCUIT

The interval training circuit is a course which we regularly set up on our practice field. It requires a minimum of space and equipment, provides a variety of experience and exercise to players, and can be used with any age group. The object, as always, is to create interesting and new ways of getting in shape. Since only four of these eight stations are with the ball, you may want to create other ideas for more. This circuit may be easily administered by one coach.

The Interval Training Circuit is easy to set up and to monitor. By the time a player has been through it twice, he'll know the state of his conditioning!

Stations

1) Shuttles 5-10-15-20 yards
2) Dribble 3 cones (5 yards apart)
3) Over-under hurdles (8 yards apart)
4) Pass ball against benches — turn and sprint to other bench.
5) Ball juggling.
6) Heading. Partner tosses ball, which is headed. Header sprints around cone, and back for another header.
7) Situps.
8) Pushups.

Conditions

A. Each player works a minimum of 30 seconds at each station. Try to build up to 60 seconds or longer.
B. Two repetitions for each group of two at each station. Partner may rest.
C. Fifteen seconds to change stations.

A PHYSICAL TEST

A little-known fact about Pele is that his vertical jump was 41 inches, a remarkable feat in itself. No wonder he was able to control so many air balls! Many people have asked my teams for a physical test, one which measures not only such factors as the vertical jump, but other important physical attributes of the modern player. Our test can be used by advanced youth, high school, college, and amateur teams, as well as by other professionals.

Here are the nine events in our test. They measure speed, agility, strength, coordination, and stamina. Although it is possible to do so, it is not recommended that the testing be done in the same day. It is suggested that you test in the following order:

EVENT	TEAM AVERAGE	COMMENT
1) 15 min. run	2 miles 221.13 yards	General endurance
2) Agility run	16.5 seconds	Changing body movement, direction
3) 40 yard dash	4.97 seconds	Quickness
4) 30/40 yard dash (backward)	5.6/7.2 seconds	Coordination
5) Chin-ups	10.1	Upper body strength
6) Vertical jump	21.08 inches	Leg power
7) Standing broad jump	7 feet 6 inches	Leg power
8) 1 minute/2 minute situps	47.33/74.5	Abdominal strength and endurance
9) 300 yard strength run	44.06 seconds	Strength of heart to withstand work

The quality vertical jump. A must for any defender.

Pele set an example. So must the ideal youth coach.

CHAPTER SEVEN

INCREASING YOUR UNDERSTANDING

INCREASING YOUR UNDERSTANDING

What is the ideal youth coach?

Philosophically, he can spot strengths and weaknesses in players, inspire players to want to improve themselves without coaching. He can plant in players the seed of modern ideas and concepts about the game instead of old yarns about "how the game was played when I was your age". He can appreciate the need for developing total players who can do *all* tactical jobs within the team; he is organized, disciplined, knowledgeable, and concerned about *growth* and *youth* — and that we learn by winning *and* by losing.

What are the assets and deficiencies of your players?

Each coach must constantly assess the good and the bad qualities of each player, and work to improve weaknesses. It may seem almost too simple, but often youth coaches deal only with praise (so as not to discourage) and others may use only criticism (to motivate players to new heights). Praise openly, criticise privately, no matter what the level. You don't have to criticise most players. They know what and when they've done wrong, though they may not know why. "Let me show you another way of beating the opponent in the tackle." is more instruction than "That's no way to tackle!" No two players have the same needs. Know the players' problems and work with them. Also, there are times when generalities will get the point across: "When we're coming out of our defensive third of the field, we're lagging behind, as if we're afraid we may lose the ball."

Can you give some ideas about achieving success as a coach?

The coach shapes the team by the players he selects for the team. Considerations must be given to skill, tactical intelligence, physical capabilities, and psychological character. This is a brief summary of team recruitment.

Secondly, the coach should remember his responsibility for the development of the complete training program on and off the field; that is, the physical and mental preparation for winning games. Effective use of time requires organization. Your training must be specific to team needs, and must induce competition, enthusiasm, and variety. Do not train just for the sake of training. Be flexible enough to recognize pitfalls in the method selected or in the results of training exercises. Change them if they need change.

Grid training is also an effective method not only in organizing your team, but in simulating game situations.

Training off the field simply means becoming as aware as possible of your players. There is no need to pry into their lives, for this will imply mistrust, and you can never recover from this negative feeling in players. Knowing where they are mentally will help you. Don't play amateur psychologist, but don't be afraid to help someone with a problem.

Four versus four in small confined space. It develops technique under pressure. Players like it.

The success of your recruitment and training is measured by your ability to coach on the day of the game. Selecting the proper team, mapping out an effective tactical plan, (with possible revisions) plus an ability to see what is happening in the game are all requisites.

In summary, the coach is responsible for all aspects of the team, and must seek a proper blend between all areas of the team organization.

You have been selected All-Star coach and must trim squad from 25 to 15 in 4 sessions. **How do you do it?**

Your objectives must be:

(1) Getting the 11 best players that will perform together most effectively and efficiently in a short period of time.

(2) Assessing the abilities of all the players (small side games of many touches that allow them to display attacking and defensive qualities and intelligence).

(3) Selecting four substitutes that can add the necessary balance and depth to your squad in case of injury or tactical changes. These four players must certainly fill all necessary changes possible — a goalkeeper? A defender; an attacking midfielder; a forward; versatile players that can play several positions.

(4) Identifying your *key players* around whom you will build the team. A central defender, goalkeeper, midfielder, forward — these are your best players. Which of the remaining 20-21 players best complement them? If it is a great header of the ball at centerforward, who can get crosses in to him? If you have a speedy winger, who can pass balls through to him from midfield or defense?

Look at the results of individual's efforts. Does he keep possession? Does he commit defenders? Does he win tackles? Does he appear relaxed and under control? Is he aggressive or passive? Confident or shy? These are obvious traits. You the coach must assess them quickly and make the right decision.

How do you break down the man-to-man marking, sometimes used by opponents?

Man-to-man marking in soccer is a high-risk maneuver, and certainly not recommended for lower levels of competition. If this tactic is used against you, spectacular and frequent goal-scoring chances can be created by using the following:

1. Double Passes (Wall Passes). Players can be sprung loose from tight marking through simple wall passes. Remember that when players are closely watched, areas of the field are left open.

2. Running off the ball. Movement is the soul of the attack. Players must run cleverly by changing speeds and occasionally using sheer speed to obtain the needed step on the opponent. Clever running also consists of appearing unconcerned about "being marked out of the game." Then, when your opponent momentarily loses concentration, you're gone!

Your team is caught offside 3-4 times. What is the remedy? What is wrong?
Attacking players must simply be *alert* to defensive tactics. Concentration is required by the attacking players to not carelessly breakdown attacking movements by being left in offside positions. Being offside usually frustrates everyone in the game, including the coach. Do not dwell on it, but solve it. Forward players can expose teams who consistently try to pull them offside with their own tactics. For example:

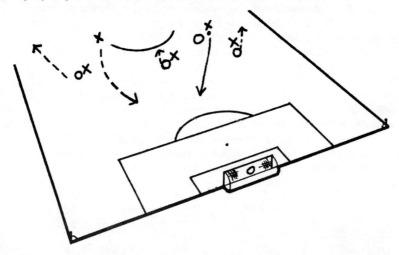

As the defense rushes forward to pull offside trap — a player runs from deep position into space where ball is being played!

Just be alert and don't be lazy. Offside is not always bad. There have been a lot of *"offside"* goals which *have won games*. Don't be afraid to score some of them.

How do you play on a narrow field?
My experiences all over America suggest that most high school and some college soccer games are played on narrow fields (because they play that other American game on it!). Narrow fields obviously create coaching problems for both teams. The game is about finding, creating, and playing into space. On small fields we must use individual movements to open spaces.

Long unimaginative passes are even more predictable on small fields. Tight ball control and razor-sharp combination play between teammates can break down even the tightest, most compact defense. Encourage your team to have patience in defense and midfield when the opponent is organized in their defense and to be alert for the counterattack before they can retreat into the small defensive third.

You are playing a team you have never seen. How do you prepare?
Be honest with your squad. Lift their spirits, don't "con" them into believing they are better than the opponent. The reality is that "we can beat anyone on a given day". Be positive about your strengths. *They* must stop us! Prepare tactical plans that can be instituted *if* any of the following occur: i.e. — fast wingers; big tall centerforward; playmaking midfielder— what we will do if this happens tomorrow? You can still make detailed alternatives that the entire team is prepared to accept and institute if required in the match.

111

What does it take to become a good professional player in America?

1. *Fundamental game skills* are most important. "Standing skills" develop confidence at first, but must be tested in motion. The world is full of "wooden players". Don't be one of them.

2. *Exceptional athletic ability* is the single most important reason for the measurable success of a Kyle Rote. His skills with a ball can probably be duplicated by thousands of young players, but he has overcome this handicap by exploring all of his natural ability through training and a positive attitude.

3. *A properly balanced psychological inventory.* Simply, this means having one's priorities in order. I have known some great players who were their own worst enemy.

4. *Ability to improvise under pressure.* Soccer's skills are few, but you won't know which one to use, when, or for how long, until the ball comes. I once heard of a 13-year-old goalkeeper who rolled the ball backward in the penalty-area to his own fullback near the goal. He did it because no one was open, and there was limited movement on the field, and it seemed the best thing to do. This is the kind of improvisation which opens up the game and the minds of its players. Most players explore few of the options that are available to them.

Ian Wood, the San Jose Earthquakes' Most Valuable Player, knows what it takes to be a professional soccer player.

Now that you've learned more about soccer, don't forget to tell others about it.